IMAGES
of America

SURFING IN NEW SMYRNA BEACH

IMAGES
of America

SURFING IN NEW SMYRNA BEACH

Kate Cumiskey

ARCADIA
PUBLISHING

Published by Arcadia Publishing
Charleston, South Carolina

Library of Congress Control Number: 2009936039

For all general information contact Arcadia Publishing at:
Telephone 843-853-2070
Fax 843-853-0044
E-mail sales@arcadiapublishing.com
For customer service and orders:
Toll-Free 1-888-313-2665

Visit us on the Internet at www.arcadiapublishing.com

This book is for Mike Martin, Buddy Wright, Skipper Eppelin, Gordon Smith, and Randy Richenberg.

CONTENTS

ACKNOWLEDGMENTS

We grow, as it were, nostalgic. We remember and reminisce. We talk about it and answer if asked. That is after all what history is all about. And who does not, in their heart of darkness, heart of light, wish for the chance to do it all again?

When I looked—when I really, really looked—this is what I found out about surfers: they are the ultimate time travelers. They have found the secret to timelessness, continuity, connectivity, and singularity. Out on the ocean, the next set might bring a wave which mimics exactly that perfect ride from when you were, say, 15, and all you had on your mind was the girl who sat in front of you in science class, when you'd be able to drive, if you could stay out until 10. And the waves roll in, and there you are 15 again. The world is your oyster. Some of the guys, a very, very few, managed to become the perfect cosmic travelers. They live with their memories with few regrets. Every day they live, work, play, and surf. They are professionals. Unlike what one might think—that they represent arrested development—they are timeless and mature. They look over the horizon in both directions and smile. This book is for them—and this town is so lucky to have them here. They've graciously contributed to this book and made it worlds better than I could have alone. They know who they are, but here are the names of everyone who helped, with a low bow to all: Mike Martin, Buddy Wright, Charley Baldwin, Skipper Eppelin, Gordon Smith, Randy Richenberg, Gene and Suzanne Varano, Frank Marshall, Rusty Davis, Bill Davis, Isabel McLaughlin, Robert Wolfe, Mike Clancy, Sonny Yambor, Mimi Hall and Tom Wheeler, Kelsi Johnson, Laura Duran Davis, Dan Hughes, Kem McNair, Vicki Van Dorn, Bill Whatley, Mikel Cumiskey, Evan Magee, Marshall Hughes, Shaman Burton, John Coffin, Joan Westhrin, and Marie Goodrich.

INTRODUCTION

I cannot pen a better introduction to the history of surfing in New Smyrna Beach than to begin with the words of Association of Surfing Professionals founding member and New Smyrna native Mike Martin. He shared these remarks at the dedication of the New Smyrna Beach Surfing Monument at the terminus of Flagler Avenue, referred to as "Main Street," on the Atlantic shore at New Smyrna Beach in 2001:

During his voyage of discovery in 1777, Captain Cook was in Tahiti, when he wrote the following passage in his journal:

> On walking one day about Matavi Point . . . I saw a man paddling in a small canoe, so quickly and looking about him with such eagerness . . . as to command all my attention. He went out from the shore 'til he was near the place where the swell begins to take its rise and paddled before it with great quickness, 'til he found that it had acquired sufficient force to carry his canoe before it.
>
> He then sat motionless and was carried along at the same swift rate as the wave, 'til it landed him upon the beach. Then he started out, emptied his canoe and went in search of another swell.
>
> I could not help concluding that this man felt the most supreme pleasure, while he was driven on, so fast, and so smoothly by the sea.

Myself and the other surfers who have dedicated this monument, along with the surfers that it is dedicated to, have all shared in that feeling . . . of a most supreme pleasure.

The monument is being mounted here, at Flagler Avenue, through the courtesy of the City of New Smyrna Beach, and the Community Redevelopment Agency, in hopes that the general public, and all who visit here, will be able to understand the conclusion that Captain Cook felt centuries ago; that people can feel supreme pleasure in the simple act of riding a wave to shore.

The history of modern surfing here in New Smyrna Beach goes back only to the early 1960's and very few people ride waves in canoes anymore. However, in those forty years we have seen an endless variety of longboards, shortboards, and catamarans, all ridden to shore by an endless variety of personalities. This beautiful wooden surfboard that Charley Baldwin has carved stands here as a symbol of surfing history, but the history of surfing is the history of the people who surfed.

Surfing is not the major thing that all those people have done with their lives, but for many of us it is the link that has bonded us together for a significant portion of our lives. The first surfers I ever saw were right here, just a few yards from where we stand now. Some of them are here today, like Skipper Eppelin, Ron Dreggors, Charlie Lyons and Jim and Gordon Smith. All of these guys are still my friends today and they were all involved in the creation of this monument, for the same reason I wanted it to happen. To have good friends for forty years is a special thing. It mostly seems to happen in small towns like New Smyrna Beach, or when you share a lifestyle like surfing. Many more good friends have moved here later in their lives, and have fit right in, because they were surfers too. Like Wes Dykes, who has taken the lead in the design and completion of the monument, and all the rest who all got involved with the Surfari Club to promote the image of surfing.

To be from New Smyrna Beach, and be a surfer, has been a blessing for me. A lot of us who feel the same way would like to give this monument back to our town. To say thanks for letting us grow up and surf here.

But this monument is not just for surfers from New Smyrna Beach, or Florida, We dedicate this monument to all the surfers of the East Coast of America, from Miami to Maine, who share our pride in being East Coasters. There are several statues and monuments in California commemorating our sport, but to my knowledge this is the first on the Eastern Seaboard. I congratulate the Smyrna Surfari Club and everyone involved for initiating this historic milestone, which is long overdue.

Sometimes it seems like surfing is really crowded, especially to us old-timers, because no one among us could have ever imagined the popularity that surfing would grow to enjoy. When I began surfing you could not buy a surfboard in New Smyrna, you had to go to Daytona Beach to a surf shop. Today you can go to five different surf shops of your choice. And you don't have to buy a surfboard from California or Cocoa Beach. You can get Randy Richenberg, or CB, or Orion, or Erie or half a dozen other manufacturers to build a board for you right here.

When I began surfing we were all self-taught and the only way to learn was by trial and error. Now you can get private lessons, or sign up for Jimmy Lane's Surf School, where hundreds of kids have learned the fundamentals of ocean safety. And if you want to compete in a surfing contest, this has been the place since 1967. The Eastern Surfing Association and National Scholastic Surfing Association both have busy schedules, and the Amateur Athletic Union holds its National Scholastic Titles here every year. The era of video has led professional surfing away from mainland America in the last ten years, but history will record that the last Association of Surfing Professionals World Tour event held on the East Coast was the Aloe-Up Cup of 1989, right here in New Smyrna Beach.

New Smyrna Beach surfers have set a standard of competitive excellence ever since the early 1970s, when Kem McNair and Charley Baldwin won their East Coast titles. Charley continued winning pro events into the 1980s and became the first New Smyrna Beach surfer inducted into the East Coast Hall of Fame. He was followed by Isabel McLaughlin, who was the United States Women's Surfing Champion in 1974. Ross Pell won two East Coast professional titles in the 1980s and Ron Hope was runner-up in the last year that an Association of Surfing Professionals-East champion was crowned.

The hot young Smyrna surfers of today are the beneficiaries of the family atmosphere that connects all those generations. When a judge from Hawaii asked me about Aaron Cormican one of the most popular surfers on video, I said, 'How could he not be a good surfer, when both his parents, Zetta and Dale were?' I travel a lot and I can tell you that the surfers of the world know where New Smyrna Beach is!

In all these ways, I believe that the sport of surfing has given something back to our town. And I believe that the surfers of New Smyrna Beach have earned their right to inherit this small spot on the beachfront where this monument will stand, looking out over all who surf here, remembering all who surfed here before, and standing in wait for those generations of surfers who are yet to come.

One

THE PIONEERS

The surfers seen on the next pages are New Smyrna Beach's surfing pioneers. They are referred to as "pioneers" because they truly embody the word. Navigating uncharted territory, they paved the way for those soon to follow—first a select few, then multitudes. There is no possible way, as with all pioneers, that they could have seen into the future or known the effects of their actions. They were young, strong, reckless, and confident.

When these young men first took to the water off Coronado Beach (which is what the island portion of New Smyrna was called in those days; indeed, that name can still be seen on churches, schools, and the like), they caught and rode waves on heavy canvas and rubber air mats encircled by rope. They pulled the mats behind them through slough, over sandbar, to the "outside break," caught waves, and rode them to the beach, then repeated the cycle. Eventually they started standing up on the mats. In order to make this work, they had to blow them up extra hard. By this time, the eyes of the town were upon them—anxiously so. With its stellar lifeguard corps (undeniably the source of the town motto "World's Safest Bathing Beach"), something had to be done, as the guards were getting tired of waving and whistling them in. The boys clearly were not about to give up their fun. An agreement was arrived at; the powers that be at city hall agreed to let the trio sign waivers—hold harmless agreements—which stated the guards would not call them in, and in return the city would not be held responsible for their safety while enjoying the waves.

Shortly thereafter, Skipper Eppelin saw his first surfboard, and his first surfer, off Daytona Beach in front of the Lido Motel. Arrangements were made, boards were acquired, and surfing came to New Smyrna Beach. Thanks to those teenage boys, the town would never be the same.

This is the first known photograph of surfers on New Smyrna Beach. Taken in the winter of 1962, the surfers are, from left to right, Skipper Eppelin, Mickey Boucher, and Buddy Wright. Behind them is Buddy's Willys Jeep, still in his garage at Bethune Beach today. To the right is Buddy's father's work truck for Wright Mill Works on the mainland. The boys piled their huge, heavy surfboards in the back and sat on top of them in transit. For years, that truck could be seen around town piled high with surfboards topped with surfers on their way to and from the beach. The gear worn by the trio is a perfect amalgam of first surfwear. Skipper wears the cutoff jeans many surfers would wear in the early days before "baggies," or board shorts, became available in the area. Mickey has on a "beaver tail," a thick neoprene suit designed for scuba diving, which zipped up the front to the neck and snapped closed between the legs in front. Buddy wears what he calls "bun huggers," a 1950s-era swimsuit. (Courtesy of Buddy Wright.)

This picture was taken in the summer of 1965 at Fourteenth Street about a mile south of Main Street and 3 miles south of the inlet. That was the designated surfing area at the time. Rollins College had a beach house back then; Robert Wolfe believes it is condominiums today. Pictured from left to right are Buddy Wright, Cheryl Swan, Richard Parker, Susan Neilsen, and Robert Wolfe. Wolfe relocated to California in 1988, when he had an opportunity to work for the *Orange County Register* newspaper. It was a tough decision after a lifetime in Florida. He has described his relocation as being similar to the sound a plant makes as it is torn from the ground, the roots snapping and breaking as it is being pulled. In hindsight, it was the best move for him and his family. (Courtesy of Robert Wolfe.)

This is the full image of the cover photograph. It is the second image taken that day; there is but one copy of the first. It hangs over Buddy Wright's fireplace. There was a retake because David "Tick" Parker made an obscene gesture. The logos on the white jackets of members were taken from Skipper Eppelin's Harbour Banana Model surfboard. As Buddy told Mike Martin in an interview for his column in the daily journal *Wavelength* in March 1984, "The Smyrna Surf Club ended when we took the treasury and went to Hawaii in 1966." Those who went to Hawaii

stayed with New Smyrna surfer and friend Art Christensen. Members are, from left to right, Ed Vogt, Buddy, Richard Parker, Robert Wolfe, Bruce Harris, Charlie Lyons, Billy Johnston, Pete Blanchet, Eugene Facey, David "Tick" Parker, John Harvey, Lloyd Dreggers, Jim Smith, Bob Kade, Skip Eppelin, Ron Dreggors, Gordon Smith, and Don Jolly. Buddy and Gordon are founding and current members of the Smyrna Surfari Club. (Courtesy of the Smyrna Surfari Club.)

The most fantastic array of great surfing photography ever presented. Exclusive helicopter film footage taken directly alongside the world's best surfers. See surfing history being made as more surfers disappear shooting the tube and then re-appear on film than has ever been shown before. Here is perhaps the greatest cast ever assembled . . . in what is certainly one of the great films of all times.

See the World's greatest Surfers surf at:

CALIFORNIA
MALIBU
RINCON
SWAMIS
REDONDO BEACH BKW'R.
BROOKS STREET
TRESTLES
WIND & SEA
WEDGE
SANTA CRUZ

TUESDAY, NOV. 10 – 7 P.M. 1962

Florida Premiere

SMYRNA THEATER

2 Hours In Magnificent Color

Admission $1.00 At Door

HAWAII
PIPE LINE
HALEIWA
SUNSET
WAIMEA
KAUNALA BAY
MAKAHA

About the time this film was shown at the local theater, the pioneers had been to Daytona and rented boards to try out and were busy acquiring their first surfboards. Surfing in Hawaii and California had been happening for years—it came late to New Smyrna Beach. (Courtesy of Mike Martin.)

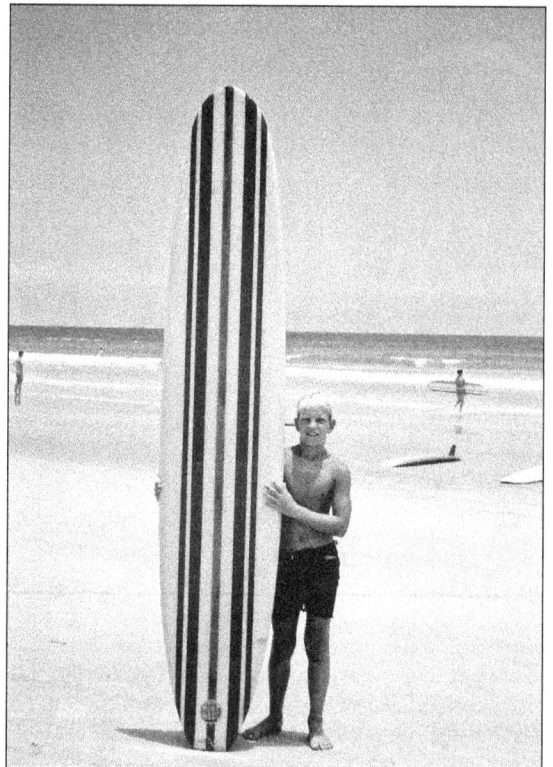

Tick Parker poses with his board in the summer of 1963, a few months after the first surfboards appeared in New Smyrna. Note the boards on the beach and the surfer checking out the waves, as well as the bystander to the left. Surfing, at this point, had come to town. (Courtesy of Buddy Wright.)

"ROOTS"   '63

A happy Mike Martin poses near his house south of town, near Twenty-seventh Avenue, with a board borrowed from David Meck. It was a "tiki," a pop-out board available in those days at department stores such as Montgomery Ward. In a classic surf tale, Mike tells how he looked up to Skipper Eppelin, Buddy Wright, and Gordon Smith. When his mother took him to buy a surfboard in Daytona Beach, they spotted the trio outside a surfshop. Buddy said to Mike, "Hey kid, lookin' for a surfboard?" They had been in Daytona to sell Skipper's surfboard, a Gordon and Smith, and Mike spent the ride home talking his mother into it. Purchasing that board, Mike gained entry into the fellowship of his heroes as well as a surfboard and friends for life. He still calls Skipper his idol. (Courtesy of Mike Martin.)

That is a "grommet" (an adolescent surfer) holding a surfboard. The other may be propped, or the tail (end of the board containing the skeg, or a fin, on the bottom rear) may be dug into the sand. These old surfboards weighed upwards of 40 pounds. Surfers often carried them two at a time, one person tucking two noses under his arms, the other between the two tails. (Courtesy of Mike Martin.)

This photograph of John Biddle in the early 1960s driving north on the beach is an excellent illustration of the convenience for surfers of living on a drive-on beach. Those racks holding his surfboard look homemade. Notice the surfer riding to the beach, right foot to the rear of the board. This is a "regular" stance. Left foot on the tail would be "goofy foot." (Courtesy of Buddy Wright.)

These photographs of Buddy Wright in 1966 show confidence and style. Buddy, Gordon Smith, and Skipper Eppelin learned to surf by trial and error. As Gordon and Buddy told Mike Martin for *Wavelength*, "We were isolated here so we had to teach ourselves the basics . . . there was no one to watch and learn from." By the time these photographs were taken, they had learned quite a bit. Meeting Steve Nielsen in 1963 had an impact on all three. He had been to California and Hawaii and encouraged them to travel. This resulted in safaris to Cocoa, where they saw "Murph the Surf" cross stepping. Until then, they had been shuffling to the nose of their boards. This was the beginning of learning from other surfers. They, in turn, would be mentors to surfers like Mike Martin. (Both photographs by Mickey Boucher, courtesy of Buddy Wright.)

Parker

Blanchet

Johnson

Galbraith

Zeppelin

Howell

Wright

Lyons

Clancy

Christensen

Biddle

Ben Roc ← Hawaii

Saunders ← Air Force

Neilson ← U.O. Florida

High School

Big Surf

Galbraith } same

Wright

Zeppelin

Parker

Smith

Blanchet

Lyons

Christensen

Johnston

Clancy

Hot Dog

Wright } same

Zeppelin

Galbraith

Smith — Biddle

Parker

Blanchet

Lyons

Clancy

Johnson

Christensen — is this that little guy with the bleached hair —

As often happens with kids in school, Buddy Wright's mind sometimes wandered during class. This list of local surfers was covertly penciled in biology class. First he listed the local surfers, adding off to the right three who were out of town. Then he divided the surfers into two categories, "Big Surf" and "Hot Dog." Under these, surfers are listed in descending order of Buddy's opinions of who was the best in big surf, who was the best in more typical New Smyrna conditions. These days, surfers who are good at "hot dogging" would be considered old school, displaying fluid and playful style on longboards and smoothly executing maneuvers like hanging ten, cheater fives, or headstands. Notice Buddy considers himself in the top on both categories, though apparently slightly better at hot dogging than big surf. There are few New Smyrna surfers who would dispute either claim. (Courtesy of Buddy Wright.)

From left to right, Donnie Hales, Mike Martin, and Jan Mikulak stand in front of Mike's 1961 Studebaker Lark, purchased from Charley Baldwin's dad, which he would later drive to California on his first West Coast surf trip. He holds a trophy from his first contest. Mike would go on to become a founding member of the Association of Surfing Professionals, a head judge on the professional surfing circuit, and author of the definitive contest surfing rules worldwide. (Courtesy of Mike Martin.)

Mike is having some fun in this 1967 photograph that he calls "weird hand signals." He looks pretty comfortable on that board, making surfing look easy. It is not. Mike surfed far south of the island's main street, Flagler Avenue, at Twenty-seventh Avenue with his friends. Twenty-seventh Avenue was his "Home Break." (Courtesy of Mike Martin.)

Art Christensen isn't pictured on the cover, and here is why: shortly after graduating from New Smyrna Beach Senior High School and receiving a low draft number, he volunteered for the navy. His duty station was on Oahu. Buddy Wright, Skipper Eppelin, and Gordon Smith stayed with him there on an epic surf trip. (Courtesy of Art Christensen.)

This is a copy of Art's orders to "report to Makaha Beach every morning at 0800 thru the week of competition (17 Dec to 24 Dec) with the Armed Forces Surfing Team." The first of the New Smyrna surfers to live in Hawaii, Art was assigned to compete in the Makaha International Surfing Meet and Competition in December 1966. (Courtesy of Art Christensen.)

Two

LIFESTYLE

Everyone loves the beach. For many people across America, the beach is a vacation playground. For a select few, including surfers in New Smyrna Beach, it is home. And when people love their home, they take care of it. Surfers feel strongly about care of the town, the surrounding environment, the ocean, and the beach. The beach attitude and the beach feeling permeate everything about the town from the restaurants along the beach (shoes optional) to first period at the local high school (wet baggies and flip-flops.) Although condominiums dot the shore, "snow birds" (Northerners) flock in October, and tourists flood the streets, New Smyrna is still New Smyrna. One of the things apparent in researching this book is the pervasiveness of the timeless element of the town. A unique place, some photographs taken a hundred years ago are easily mistaken for current. That is nice. Equally photographs of many of the surfers remind local mothers, particularly, that the picture of a grommet from 1967 could be the picture of a grommet from 2009. This is a lovely element to a community—created by a sport with zero negative impact—that is shown in this chapter. What one gives up to live in New Smyrna Beach pales in comparison with what one gains. And be aware that living here as anywhere is a conscious choice; it is simplistic to view a community as one that survives on tourist dollars (inaccurate) or one open to the whims of the modern world. As with any culture, it is most receptive to outsiders who take the time and thought to learn and honor the local code. Here that involves respect for place and for people, a simple enough concept often forgotten by visitors. Nothing makes a local madder than dangerous behavior on the part of a visitor, such as jaywalking a busy beachside street or falling asleep near a lifeguard tower thinking the guard is a babysitter. And in the water, surfers need to defer to local rules.

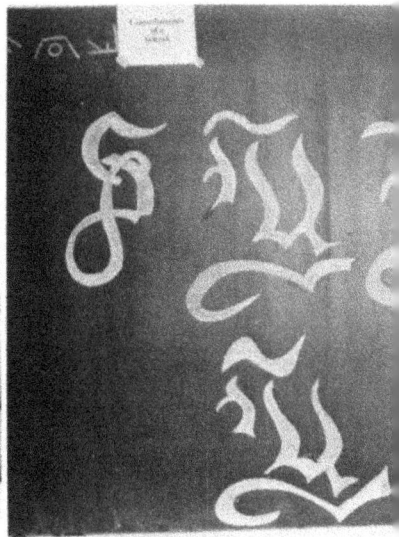

This photograph from the 1968 *Smyrnan*, the yearbook at the local high school, is a perfect opener for a chapter on lifestyle. Rusty Davis (left) and Steve Whaley hold Nancy Preston atop Rusty's surfboard. He says, "The board is a 1968, 10' 2" "Step-down" made by Southcoast Surfboards. I believe it was an import from Australia, though I've not been able to locate any reference to that particular board on line. I got it at the old Daytona Surf Shop (Main Street) on sale for $125.00 new." He cleaned fish for a summer to earn the money. Those were the days. Interestingly, in the

1968 yearbook, there were several fantastic surfing photographs, and many other beach shots, as will be seen. By contrast, in the 1980 yearbook, there were zero surfing shots. To be fair, there are more and more students as the years go by and less yearbook space. That said, in the late 1960s and early 1970s, surfing was a priority for students as well as staff. Until very recently, the high school was perched on an island between mainland and beachside, tantalizingly close to surf. (Courtesy of Rusty Davis.)

Passing this photograph around among locals in an experiment prior to publication to find out if people would find it dated, the response was universally the same: "I know where that is! That's the view north on Riverside Drive on the mainland." It is true, but this photograph was taken more than a hundred years ago. It looks exactly the same today. (Courtesy of the Southeast Volusia Historical Society.)

This photograph of the flood of 1910 on the mainland illustrates that New Smyrna is a town subject to capricious elements of nature. Both houses still stand and look none the worse for the wear. Still, locals learn to live with the sometimes-violent tides, and surfers often take advantage of them. (Courtesy of the Southeast Volusia Historical Society.)

Heavily advertised, New Smyrna Beach is still considered a playground by many. Notice the size of the advertisement compared to the man standing below it. This billboard promotes the town in the late 1950s and early 1960s in Cape Canaveral. It is interesting that one of the selling points is "adequate schools." (Courtesy of the Southeast Volusia Historical Society.)

A courtesy to visitors, the town council donated this tide clock purely for outsiders. Any surfer or seaman worth his salt knows all about the tides and what they do to the waves particularly. And all locals know that the tides on the river (also the Intracoastal Waterway) are two hours behind the Atlantic Ocean. (Courtesy of the Southeast Volusia Historical Society.)

The New Smyrna style is evidenced
by one of the photographs from the
1968 yearbook. An anonymous student
enjoys the natural bench provided by
a palm tree, probably in a local park.
Students to this day in New Smyrna
have to learn to ignore the paradisiacal
aspects of the town and concentrate
on their studies—not always easy
to do. (Courtesy of Rusty Davis.)

This shrimp boat is typical of the ones
seen off New Smyrna in early mornings.
Shrimping was a source of income for
many locals, as was fishing. While still a
source of fresh seafood, the local shrimp
boats are fewer and fewer, as the economy
dictates. (Courtesy of Rusty Davis.)

New Smyrna Fla
Sand Dunes & Atlantic Ocean

The dunes at New Smyrna Beach were quite built up when this photograph was taken around 1910. Although there are still wooden walkways to protect the dunes, increased human activity, including construction, as well as the caprices of Mother Nature have severely eroded the dune line on most of the beachfront. (Courtesy of the Southeast Volusia Historical Society.)

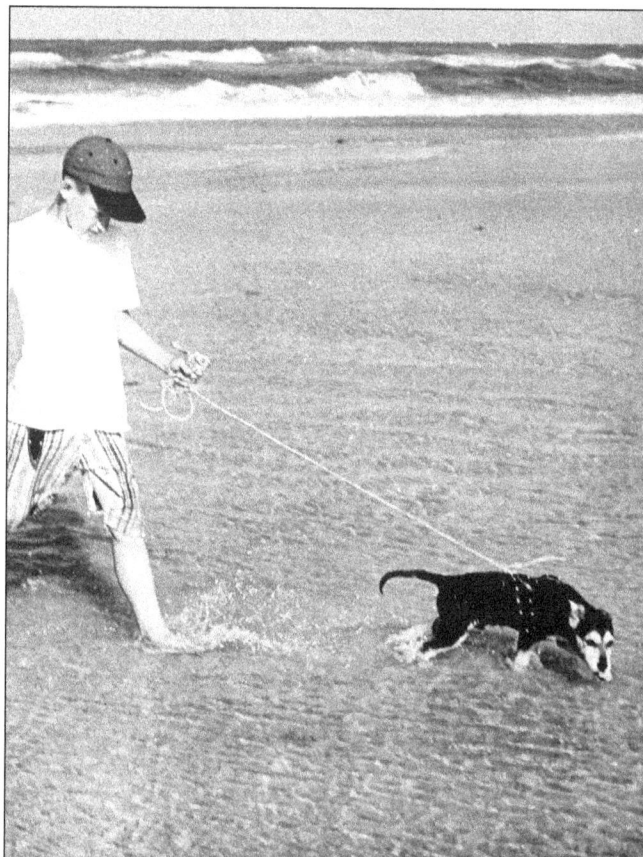

A boy walks his pet in the shore break in this picture from the 1968 *Smyrnan*. Although this might be a current scene except for the date accompanying the photograph, pets are currently allowed on the beach only north of the jetty at Smyrna Dunes Park and then only when leashed. (Courtesy of Rusty Davis.)

These two views of a party to celebrate the end of World War II show most of the town turning out, along with military personnel with their vehicles. They could have traveled from any of a number of posts and bases around the state of Florida. Parties on the beach for almost any reason, or none at all, are common. Open fires on the beach at New Smyrna have been banned for some time, and driving is now prohibited except during daylight hours. There are fire pits available during fall and winter months in several places. Keeping the beach clean is the responsibility of beachgoers as well as maintenance crews funded by taxes. However, many groups, including the Smyrna Surfari Club, regularly hold beach cleanups. (Both courtesy of the Southeast Volusia Historical Society.)

This poster advertising fishing of "all kinds" at New Smyrna dates to the 1940s. New Smyrna has long been a world-class destination for anglers. This is a double-edged sword for surfers, as they may enjoy that sport too, but fish bring in bigger fish, including sharks. Also note "a paradise for pensioners"—the town still is largely a retirement community. (Courtesy of the Southeast Volusia Historical Society.)

The view west over the north bridge down Flagler Avenue is the view toward the mainland. Residents are used to waiting for the drawbridge. There is another bridge, higher and with four lanes, a mile south at Third Avenue. Locals inevitably prefer the more aesthetically pleasing North Bridge and are philosophical about the wait when it is up for boat traffic. (Courtesy of the Southeast Volusia Historical Society.)

The annual Christmas parade, starting here at the corner of Orange and Canal Streets on the mainland, generally draws the entire town. Many youngsters participate. This station wagon sports a pair of Aloha surf racks, or "hard racks," meant to stay on a vehicle permanently. They are now vintage, expensive, and difficult to find. (Courtesy of Rusty Davis.)

A trifold brochure for a local motel advertises all the enticements of the town. Directly on "The World's Safest Bathing Beach," mom-and-pop establishments like the White Sands have unfortunately given way, for the most part, to high-rise condominiums. The beach north of Crawford Road is still pristine and without heavy development, except for a cluster of monolithic condominiums at the inlet. (Courtesy of the Southeast Volusia Historical Society.)

A lone sunbather enjoys an idyllic day at the shore. Notice the catamaran beyond the wave. That wave is a perfect tube, and spray blown back off the top indicates an offshore breeze, perfect for shaping hollow barrels. This is a decades-old picture. These days, a wave like that, particularly at the inlet, would most likely be crowded. (Courtesy of the Southeast Volusia Historical Society.)

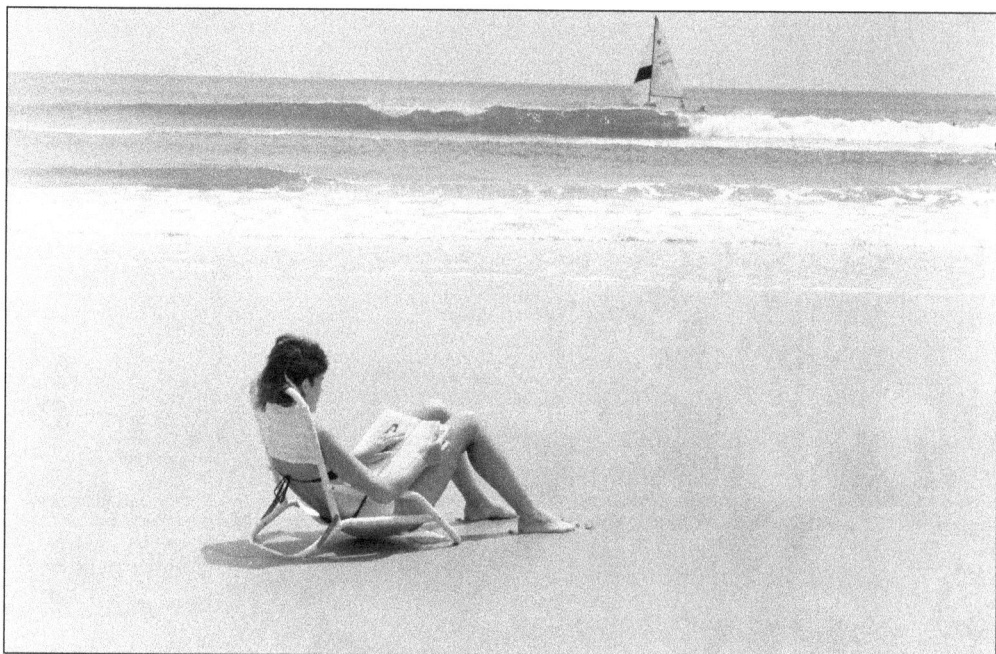

BEST BEACHSIDE ACCOMMODATIONS

FOR YOUR PLEASURE, COMFORT AND CONVENIENCE

SHANNON BY THE SEA
2800 S. ATLANTIC AVENUE
TELEPHONE 1000
EFFICIENCY APARTMENTS & MOTEL UNITS

NEW SMYRNA SHORES
S. ATLANTIC AVE. AT 18TH STREET
TELEPHONE 222-R
OCEAN FRONT EFFICIENCY APARTMENT

CORONADO DUNES
S. ATLANTIC AVE. AT 24TH STREET
TELEPHONE 1238
COTTAGE COLONY & MAID SERVICE

HILLTOP APARTMENTS
207 N. ATLANTIC AVENUE
TELEPHONE 61-J
OCEAN SIDE APARTMENTS

WHITE SANDS MOTEL
S. ATLANTIC AVE. AT 23RD STREET
TELEPHONE 1213
OCEAN FRONT MOTEL ROOMS AND APTS.

LEE-WAY APARTMENTS
S. ATLANTIC AVE. AT 8TH STREET
TELEPHONE 245-M
APARTMENTS ON THE OCEAN

This old brochure promoting the town sports stylized line drawings of tourists having fun. Most of the small, personal motels in this brochure have gone under or been overtaken by businesses who can pack in more rooms for sale or rent on a small piece of land by building up. (Courtesy of the Southeast Volusia Historical Society.)

This old postcard shows the Windbeam Inn, an establishment with an elegant dining room overlooking the Atlantic. The seawall in front jutted close to the shore, and waves often broke against the wall during winter storms. While the inn is long gone, "the Wall" was only recently removed. Sonny Yambor recalls the wooden umbrella stands that were called "Planters"—they were sponsored by the peanut company. (Courtesy of the Southeast Volusia Historical Society.)

The Breakers is a bar and restaurant perched on the north corner of the main beach ramp at the end of Flagler Avenue. It has been ravaged by many high tides in hurricanes and nor'easters, even losing the entire porch at one point. (Author's collection.)

This is an excellent view of the parking lot at the south corner of Flagler Avenue, as well as the lifeguard station, tower, and public restrooms to the right of the picture. Taken at dawn, it shows most of the town turning out for the Easter sunrise service in 1980. (Courtesy of the Southeast Volusia Historical Society.)

An older couple enjoys watching passersby and the water on a bench at the boardwalk at Flagler Avenue. In the left foreground below the railing is one of the yellow and blue rubber rafts available for rent up and down the beach at concession stands, which also rent chairs and umbrellas and sell drinks, snacks, and hot dogs. The breaking waves look perfect for riding. (Courtesy of the New Smyrna Beach Historical Society.)

Who is the surfer in this bunch? Actually both men in the middle of the group surf, but check out the break reflected in those 1980s shades. When the waves are breaking, it is hard to get a surfer to hold still on shore long enough to snap a photograph. (Courtesy of Bill Davis.)

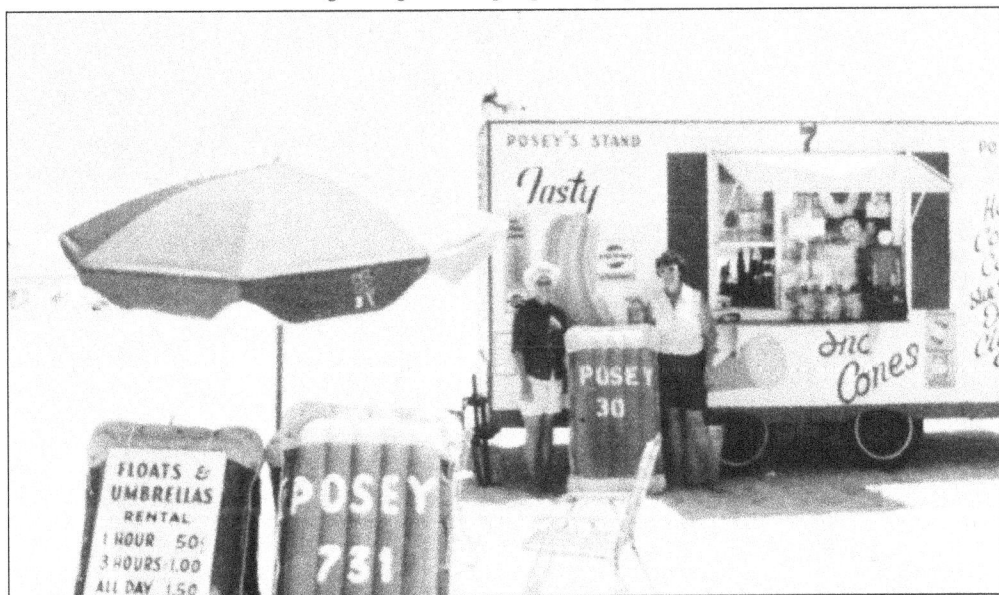

One of the benefits of a drive-on beach is that concessionaires, like the women pictured above, can park right on the beach to sell and rent their wares. Prices have gone up since this picture was taken. Those air mattresses are the same type that the surfing pioneers started with in the late 1950s. (Courtesy of Rusty Davis.)

At the northern tip of the island, Smyrna Dunes Park offers off-beach parking, facilities, and miles of elevated walkways to the inlet on both the river and ocean sides. Surfers often park when they want to surf past the time when the beach itself is closed to vehicular traffic, a half-hour before sunset. (Courtesy of the Southeast Volusia Historical Society.)

A lone surfer heads in with his longboard on a winter evening. The walk to the parking lot at Smyrna Dunes Park is often well worth it for a surfer who wants to spend time at the inlet in the uncrowded conditions after most people clear the beach. (Author's collection.)

Mikel Cumiskey Jr. was the recipient of the 2001 Smyrna Surfari Scholarship. The scholarship is given to a student club members feel promotes surfing in a positive way and who will most likely surf all his life. (Author's collection.)

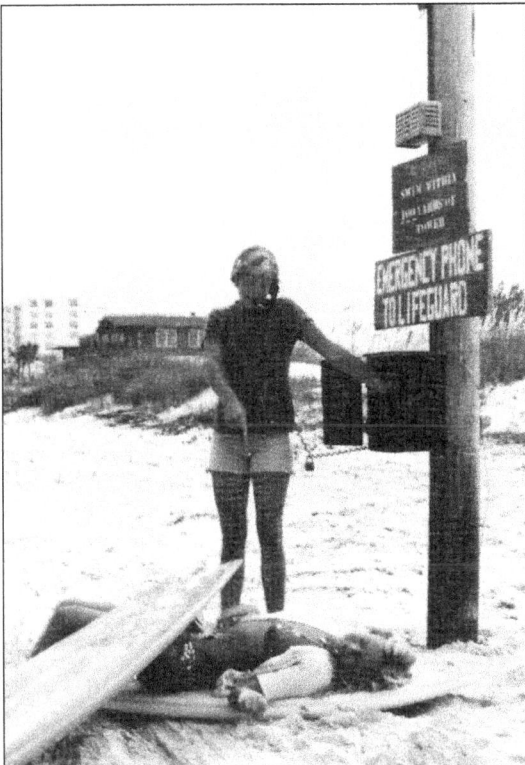

In this 1975 yearbook photograph, sisters Isabel and Cathy McLaughlin make an excellent point: always surf with a buddy. One of the things which make this "the World's Safest Bathing Beach" is, paradoxically, how dangerous the water can be. Surfers learn from a young age to hydrate, protect their skin, and sharply analyze both the conditions and their own abilities. (Courtesy of New Smyrna Beach Senior High School.)

From left to right are Randy Schwoerer, Bill O'Hara, and Ronnie Shipman. To quote Mike Martin, "Ron Shipman was the most talented 'switch-foot' surfer I ever saw. You could not detect which was his natural stance. When we judged him in pro contests, I used to subtly notify the other, out-of-town judges, 'you realize he just rode that left as a goofy-foot and his first wave was a right, as a regular foot.' I was curious about this until I finally asked Ronnie. His reply: 'When I started surfing I just thought you should change stance to face the wave, left or right. It took about two years before one of my friends said you're switching feet (actually one of the most difficult tasks to learn). So I learned how to go backside, both ways.' After that, Ron became the only surfer I ever saw who would randomly ride both lefts and rights, either forehand or backhand, so seamlessly as to be undetectable." (Courtesy of Buddy Wright.)

Three

CONTESTS

This story illustrates two elements of uniqueness of New Smyrna: The class of surfer developed here and the arc of family influence over time.

This item appeared in the paper in mid-December 1982:

> Surfing Birthdays: Last Saturday, Mike Brewer, Surfari Club cochairman enjoyed his 29th birthday by dominating the lefts at Bethune Beach where the surf was 3 to 5 feet with offshore winds. His fellow Surfaris were heard to testify that old age has not hampered his fluid style.
>
> On the same morning, the CB surf team gained its newest member when Charley and Jennifer Baldwin became the proud parents of a beautiful 8 pound daughter, Lindsey Anne. My prediction is to watch for Lindsey Anne Baldwin in the Women's Final at Cape Hatteras in 1999. December 16, 1982.

It was penned by Lindsey's godfather, Mike Martin. Mike was wrong—he underestimated Lindsey. She took the girl's title earlier than predicted, in 1996. Here is part of an essay about the victory from her yearbook:

> The horn sounded and myself and five other competitors ran into the heat. In the semifinal, which determined if I went on to the final where I could fight for the title of east coast champ, I was able to catch three good waves and I won the heat. This gave me the confidence that I may have a chance to win the title. . . . The horn sounded and the six of us (including my sister Marcie) paddled out. I couldn't help but watch the other girls. Luckily a few good waves boosted my confidence. I could hear the yelling and clapping of my friends and family on the beach. The horn sounded and the final was over. Everyone congratulated my sister and me. That night we just relaxed. The overnight wait for the results was a nail-biting event, but the next day came quickly. We headed for the awards ceremony. . . . They called sixth through third place; the remaining two spots were left to my sister and me. Marcie won second and I was the new East Coast Girls Champion. I was so happy.

This fantastic shot of Buddy Wright hanging heels off Main Street (Flagler Avenue) was taken at the first contest in New Smyrna Beach, in 1967. Buddy certainly learned quickly, considering he only started out a few years prior. Buddy still surfs whenever he can get out there. (Courtesy of Buddy Wright.)

This photograph is of Mike Tabeling, a Hobie team member, getting ready for a heat. He is reaching into his wax pocket for a bar of wax. (Courtesy of Mike Martin.)

This poster announces the second contest in New Smyrna Beach. It drew professional surfers from up and down the East Coast, including the Hobie team from Cocoa. The photograph shows Hobie team member Gary Propper next to the van before the contest. He apparently went into it fairly confident. This event was ambitious for the newly formed surf club, and according to the local paper, it drew hundreds of surfers from out of town. The surfers behaved particularly well, filling all available rooms in the area and bringing a good deal of business in. Although all members of the Hobie team rode Propper models, and Gary himself ended up inviting local grommet (and winning contestant in the midget division) Kem McNair to join the team, he was not necessarily happy to lose out in the open division to local talent. (Both courtesy of Mike Martin.)

First Annual Coronado Open

Flagler Avenue Approach

New Smyrna Beach, Fla.

Nov. 18-19, 1967 Starting 7 A.M.

$3.00 All Events ★ $4.00 After Nov. 15

SENIOR MEN'S	JUNIOR MEN'S
18 and Over	15 - 17
MIDGET'S	WOMEN'S OPEN
14 and Under	MEN'S OPEN

Check out those love beads. Miss Southland 1967, Dixie Massey, wears spike heels, a bathing suit, and a winning smile in spite of the chilly weather. The fellow behind her even has on a fur collar. The contest was held at the end of Flagler Avenue. (Courtesy of Buddy Wright.)

Local Mike Clancy accepts his trophy. This contest was a real turning point for the town of New Smyrna Beach. Area merchants were pleasantly surprised by the behavior of contestants and spectators, and the surfing world was introduced to a town and unexpected talent. New Smyrna Beach and its surfers were on the map. (Courtesy of Rusty Davis.)

Charley Baldwin, a local boy shown here getting his third-place trophy for the junior men's division, stunned everyone, including himself, by taking first in the open division. He said, "I can't believe it—never thought I'd win." This event was open to only the top three winners in the four previous contests: midgets, women, junior men, and senior men. Surfers had come from Virginia Beach and California. While the Hobie team took top honors in the senior men's competition, with Gary Propper coming in first, they lost out to Baldwin in the heavy competition of the open division. This division was open to the top three in the four previous age groups. Mike Tabeling was none too happy about it; he was seen to walk away from the awards ceremony and dump his trophy in a trash can. The next day's headline in the Daytona paper read "New Smyrna Surfers Prevail; Steal Coronado Club's Show." The first paragraph said, "Two new Smyrna Beach surfers stole the show from nationally known surfing champions in the first annual Coronado Surf Club fun contest Saturday and Sunday." (Courtesy of Mike Martin.)

This is a photograph of Jim Smith surfing Main Street around 1967. The board was a 9-foot, 4-inch Surfboards Hawaii that stolen from his yard about two weeks after this photograph. He says he is still searching for the bastard who stole his all-time favorite board. (Courtesy of Jim Smith.)

In spring of 1967, the high school's Hi-Y club held a local contest. The judges' stand was the bed of a 1954 Chevy pick-up. Check out the youngster on the nose of the board in the center of the photograph, pretending to hang 10. In the water, of course, the fin would be down, and she would be standing on the "deck." (Courtesy of Jim Smith.)

44

Jim Smith presents a trophy to the women's winner, Sue Hunter, in the Hi-Y contest. Jim was club president. Tick Parker, a "hot shot" local surfer according to Jim, holds a Hansen 50/50. That board would easily be worth several thousand dollars today. Third from the left is Mike Clancy, who won the men's division. This contest took place just north of the Crawford Road approach. The waves in the background are typical of that beach before the inlet jetty was completed. There was a high seawall between the few houses along Atlantic Avenue and the beach, and spectators could sit or stand atop the seawall, and in winter at high tide, look down into the surf. This is a section of the north beach (north of Flagler Avenue) where development has been restricted to single family homes. Although there are plenty of them between Crawford Road and Canaveral National Seashore at the southern end of the island, no condominiums ruin the small-town atmosphere between Crawford and the inlet. (Courtesy of Jim Smith.)

This photograph from Mike Martin's 1971 "Full Boogie" contest captures the vulnerability and innocence of a generation. From left to right, Mark Scarborough, Mike, Rick Tresher, and Randy Schwoerer are turned toward the camera. Janie O'Hara's column "Green Room" stated, "The waves were perfect ten to twelve feet high and very well formed. Competitors were chosen by ballot . . . judging and placing were done in a new experimental manner. The judges were permitted to discuss the rides of the contestants and decide who should go into the semi-finals and finals. No point system was used and eventually there were only five finalists, all equal in standing, with no first, second or third-place winners. Finalists were Charley Baldwin, Randy Schwoerer, David Sagraves, Randy Richenberg and Rick Tresher. . . . Everyone agreed that much had been accomplished in the progress of surfing contests and this one was voted a success. Winners and losers alike went home happy because of the fairness of the judging the warm feeling of comradeship that resulted." Mike provided this article. (Courtesy of Charley Baldwin.)

To quote Mike Martin, who brought this contest to town, "The Aloe-Up Cup, in 1988 and 1989, turned out to be the last East Coast event to be sanctioned by the ASP—the Association of Surfing Professionals. The ASP Board of Directors, including the surfer representatives, decided that the waves on the East Coast were too small and inconsistent to warrant giving points toward the ASP world title. Since then, dozens of East Coast events have been rated on the 2nd Tier/World Qualifying Series point standings. However, the surf hasn't changed so I believe we will probably never again see an ASP World Championship event on the East Coast." (Photograph by Sonny Yambor, courtesy of the Smyrna Surfari Club.)

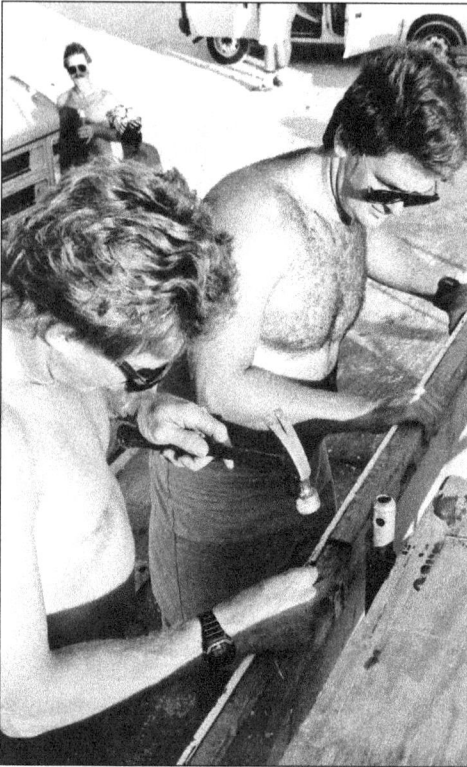

Putting on a surf contest and pulling one off smoothly is a great deal of work. Months of planning and preparation go into it, as well as days of exhausting work. Teamwork is key. For all-volunteer organizations such as the Smyrna Surfari Club and Christian Surfers, this means selflessness and dedication on the part of members. (Photograph by Sonny Yambor, courtesy of the Smyrna Surfari Club.)

Perched atop scaffolding erected for the contest, members of the Smyrna Surfari Club work the Ninth Annual New Smyrna Surfari Classic at the inlet. One of the great things about the Smyrna Surfari Club is that its members range from surfing pioneers like Gordon Smith and Buddy Wright and professionals like Mike Martin to up-and-coming youngsters. (Photograph by Sonny Yambor, courtesy of the Smyrna Surfari Club.)

In a volunteer capacity, Mike Martin selflessly offers his time as a head judge for local amateur contests time and again despite a heavy schedule with the Association of Surfing Professionals. Mike travels all over the world, but as a New Smyrna native, he always returns home. Here he is at work at the U.S. Surfing Federation Amateur Titles in Oceanside, California. (Photograph by Paul West, courtesy of Mike Martin.)

Adam Wright takes a breather while working a Surfari contest. Surfari members make beautiful trophies, and because of who they come from, the hands that made them, and the history behind those hands, they mean quite a lot to young surfers. The three boards on the left will be raffled off to raise money for the scholarship fund. (Courtesy of the Smyrna Surfari Club.)

This picture appeared under the title "When the Surf's Up" in the *Daytona News Journal* on May 19, 1968. How quickly surfing became popular in New Smyrna Beach, when the first boards arrived a mere five years before. Longboarders these days would love to lay their hands on boards like these. (Photograph by Nelle Hays, courtesy of Mike Martin.)

Surfaris always throw some fun into the contests to keep the mood light. The costume contest at the annual October Spooktackular is a highlight. There is a prize for best costume. The annual club membership photographs are often taken at the contest, too. (Courtesy of the Smyrna Surfari Club.)

50

Buddy Wright and Gordon Smith work the first Surfari contest from a picnic table on the beach. The item just showing in the right of the photograph is a cage for pulling raffle tickets, which is the same one used at Surfari contests to this day. (Courtesy of the Smyrna Surfari Club.)

One of the best things about Christian Surfers New Smyrna Beach Chapter is that they show up at nearly every surfing event in town, set up a tent, and hand out water and healthy snacks. Another is the range of events and talent at their own competitions. Kate and Bill Whatley started and run the local chapter of Christian Surfers. In the whitewater division, an adult can go out with the grommet and push them into the wave. A lot of great New Smyrna surfers get their first taste of competitive surfing in this gentle, fun environment. This is Nate Colburn, who took first place in the boys division of Before the Fall 2006. (Courtesy of Bill Whatley.)

This May 13, 1981, photograph from the *News and Observer* features, from left to right, contestants (first row) Mike Risk, Lee Schwoerer, and Kerry Pearson; (second row) Kris Walko, Kay Buhler, Lee Ann Luedeke, Rick Browning, Gary Schwoerer, and Lee Conklin. Surfing is often a family affair in New Smyrna, and the Schwoerers are the younger two of a family of surfing brothers. (Courtesy of the Smyrna Surfari Club.)

Art Christensen took this snapshot of teammates on the Armed Forces Surf Team at Makaha in the late 1960s. Art enlisted in the navy during the Vietnam War because his draft number was seven. His duty station ended up being in Hawaii—rough duty. (Courtesy of Art Christensen.)

Marcie Baldwin, younger daughter of Jennifer and Charley, shows power and style during a contest. Face it—surfing just runs in the family. (Courtesy of Charley Baldwin.)

The caption for this shot reads, "Lindsey Baldwin is smacking the lip in her final at the 1996 Easterns. The waves and weather were good that day. Five people from N.S.B. attended the Easterns." If they do well locally, contestants often travel to surf. Freesurfers, surfers who do not compete, also often travel for surf. (Courtesy of New Smyrna Beach High School.)

Todd Perry is ripping in this photograph from his heat in Cape Hatteras, North Carolina, in the 1996 East Coast championship. Cape Hatteras is one of the many places surfers visit, but locals like Todd return home happy to surf their own inlet. (Courtesy of New Smyrna Beach High School.)

"Lindsey Baldwin and Todd Perry, hanging in Hatteras at Rodanthe Pier. They were all smiles after a fun day of great surf and good times. The weather was perfect without a cloud in the sky," reads the caption for this yearbook shot. Who could ask for more? (Courtesy of New Smyrna High School.)

This item appeared in the local paper for a 1968 contest presented by Daytona Beach Junior College, now Daytona State College. The caption reads: "Winners Smiles are flashed from Don Blackwelder, tandem winner and second place men's division; Roger Shepherd, winner of men's division and paddleboard race; Mike Martin, second place paddleboard race and third place men's division. Linda Baron, winner of tandem and women's division; Sharon Van Winkle, second place tandem; Beverly Day, third place women's division and Helen Ciallella, second place women's division." Mike Martin is actually in the center, with Roger Shepherd to the right facing the camera. Mike says, "I coerced my girlfriend Sharon Van Winkle, who did not surf, to paddle out with me on the front of my board to compete in the tandem division. Roger Shepherd won everything that day." (Courtesy of Mike Martin.)

Wes Cich, the recipient of the 1999 Smyrna Surfari Scholarship, can be seen absolutely tearing it up around town when he is home visiting his parents, Suzanne and Gene Varano. Wes is a fine example of New Smyrna talent. (Courtesy of Bill Whatley.)

New Smyrnan Amy Nichol is seen here upon hearing she took the Costa Crown Series for Christian Surfers 2006. Amy is a member of the U.S. Surf Team and surfs all over the world, but her home break is still the inlet. Amy is extremely talented and bright. She always has a kind word for grommets paddling out, too; she is a great influence on up-and-coming young surfers. (Courtesy of Bill Whatley.)

Members of the Smyrna Surfari Club pause for a snapshot at the end of Lincoln Avenue on the North Beach, Gordon Smith's (second from left) home break. Many ride boards from local surfer, shaper, and Surfari member Charley Baldwin. Others ride classic boards by shapers like Jim Phillips. (Photograph by Jan Lyons, courtesy of the Smyrna Surfari Club.)

This is a Smyrna Surfari Club annual photograph, snapped before a contest at which each of these members will be hard at work all day. Members display a variety of boards, some by local shapers like Randy "Big R" Richenberg. Gene (second from right, standing) holds his Richenberg longboard. (Courtesy of the Smyrna Surfari Club.)

In this 1966 photograph taken following the Halifax Area Surfing Society Contest, Mike Martin shows off his third-place trophy and his Surfboards Hawaii tri-stringer. Mike would go on to become the most well-respected, experienced judge in the professional surfing world and one of several surfing professionals New Smyrna Beach can unashamedly boast of. The board was later stolen off the top of the car in Mike's front yard. He never saw it again. (Courtesy of Mike Martin.)

From left to right, Gene Varano, Bill Whatley (holding daughter Lilly), Steve Davis, Adam Wright, and first-place longboard winner Mikel Cumiskey Jr. pose after a Surfari Spooktackular Contest. Said Mikel years later, "I've surfed Costa Rica, Hawaii; and up and down the west coast. That trophy means more to me than all the rest." There is nothing like winning among friends and mentors. (Courtesy of the Smyrna Surfari Club.)

Four

SHOPS AND SHAPERS

In the beginning, surfers had to buy boards in Daytona Beach or send away for them. Skipper Eppelin tells how Buddy Wright sent money to California for a Bing. The shaper packed it carefully, sending Buddy the exact board he had seen in a magazine. Buddy had cut the picture out and sent it to Bing. Years later, Skipper saw a beautiful Bing hardcover book at the Surf Expo in Orlando, with a photograph of Buddy's board inside. He immediately bought a copy for Buddy and one for himself and was thrilled to learn Bing was at the Surf Expo. When he went over to talk to the master shaper and tell the story, emphasizing the care taken in filling Buddy's order, Bing Copeland replied, "Of course. We take that much care in filling all our orders." That attitude typifies the standards of the masters. Locally Randy Richenberg fills that bill. Randy surfs and shapes with love, honor, and heart. He cannot be rushed and was recently rewarded for his integrity by being elected to the position of city commissioner by an overwhelming 73 percent of his district. Many locals depend on Randy to carefully husband resources, fiscal and natural, of the town, which is a tall order. He meets it handily. And he continues to hone his skills and patiently mentor youngsters who wish to learn the art of shaping surfboards. That said, several fine shapers make their home here. Charley Baldwin must be mentioned. While Charley built a lucrative business shaping and retailing (he recently sold his surf shop, Inlet Charley's), he also gained respect as local boy made good with his fluid style of surfing in the 1960s and 1970s and is the father of two of New Smyrna's fine young surfers, Lindsey and Marcie.

These days, surf shops, which sell everything from bikinis to sunscreen, videos to skateboards, dot the town. New Smyrna's original Gordon and Smith dealer, Smyrna Surf Shack, was originally owned by Janie O'Hara and later by her brother Bill. Quiet Flight now sits on that site. Many shops and shapers have come and gone; some of their advertisements follow.

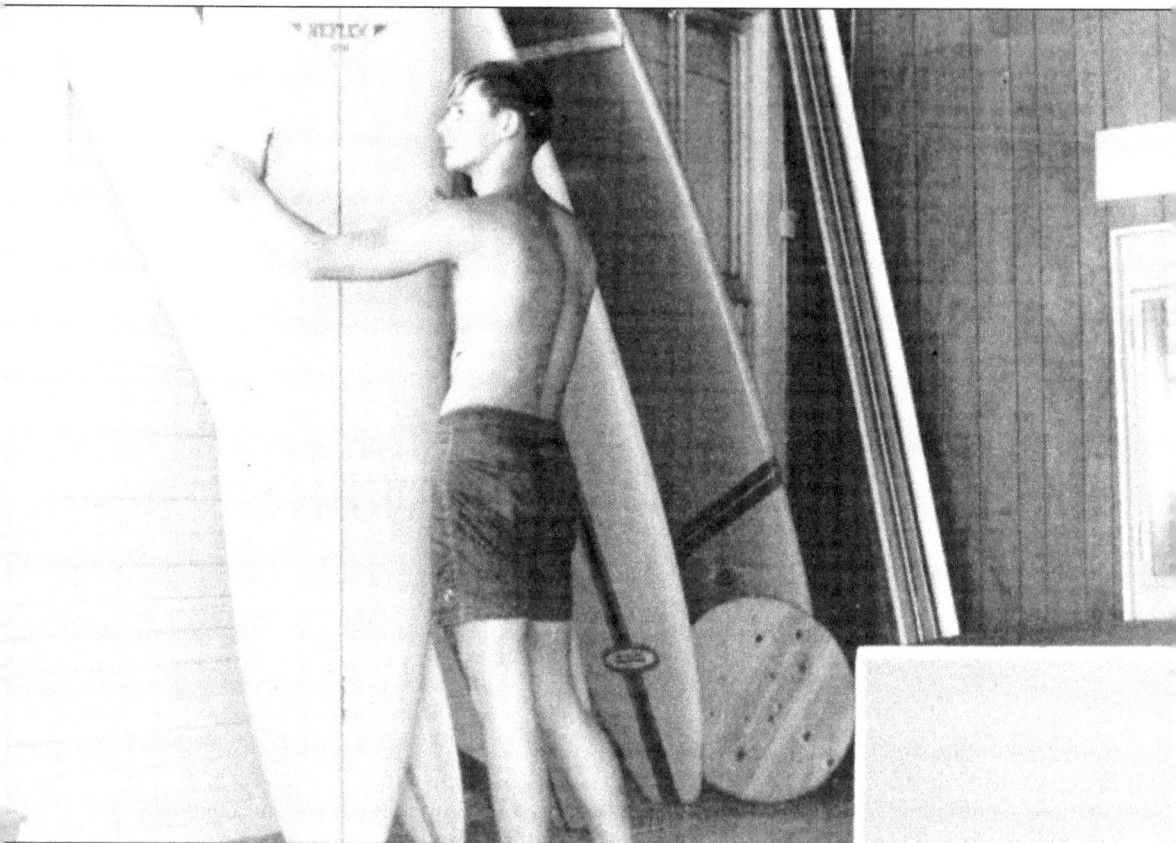

This advertisement from the 1968 *Smyrnan* yearbook for the Smyrna Surf Club, the club that followed the Coronado Surf Club, wishing seniors well, was probably taken in Janie's. Back in those days, shops sold the bare minimum equipment, before the surf industry involved clothing, advertising, media, and the like. All that can be seen are boards, and notice the vintage skim board (the round wooden disk). This one looks handmade. Perhaps the young man in the picture set it down to hold up the surfboards. Skim boards are used at low tide by tossing one over the path of a receding wave at the shoreline laterally and then running and jumping on, "skimming" along the shore on a thin sheet of water. Riders sometimes even toss them toward the shore break and pop over waves into the water. These days, like surfboards, they are available from a variety of vendors, even at the grocery store. Local paramedics call them "Slip and snaps;" they are dangerous. (Courtesy of Rusty Davis.)

Randy Richenberg, owner and operator of Richenberg Surfboards, is a master shaper and city commissioner who still finds time to get shacked. (Courtesy of Randy Richenberg.)

SMYRNA SURF SHACK INC.

Best Wishes to the Seniors of 1982.

508 Flagler Ave.
New Smyrna Beach, Fl.
427-1917

710 Third Ave.
New Smyrna Beach, Fl.
423-4622

Shop owners like Bill O'Hara often bought advertisements in the yearbooks to wish seniors well and to support the local high school. Surfing is a huge, important part of the community, and for the most part surf shops are a safe place for youngsters to hang out. There is often fierce loyalty to particular shops as well as shapers. (Courtesy of New Smyrna High School.)

Mikel Cumiskey Sr. remembers the board at the left and the one eighth from the left in the picture below being sold to brothers from Lakeland, Florida, one day when Mikel was in the shop. He was a shop rat at the Smyrna Surf Shack and did ding repair (fixing holes and cracks in surfboards) for Bill O'Hara. Conditions were dangerous for novices, well overhead. Bill asked Mikel to go out with the boys, who insisted on trying out their new surfboards, to try to keep them safe. After battling heavy surf, they caught the same wave and stood up, yelling, "We're doing it! Just like in the magazine!" dropping down the face of the wave and banging into each other all the way to the beach. They immediately sold the boards back to Bill for a fraction of what they had paid an hour before. Mikel and Bill had a tough job repairing them. (Both, author's collection.)

By the 1970s, surf shops were springing up across the island and even on the mainland. This one was actually on the North Causeway, which is across the river on the way to the mainland. Owning a surf shop is a difficult business requiring long hours. (Courtesy of New Smyrna Beach High School.)

This yearbook advertisement features Dan Nichols, David Coffee, and Kem McNair. In 1971, Kem and David Coffee opened M.C.G.'s Sun and Surf Shop on Flagler Avenue. They started building M.C.G. Surfboards. Kem was on the East Coast team to the U.S. Championships in 1970–1972 and on the East Coast team to the World Championships in Ocean Beach, California, in 1972. (Courtesy of New Smyrna High School.)

INLET CHARLEY'S SURF SHOP

Swim Wear & Beach Fashions
510 Flagler Ave.
New Smyrna Beach   Florida 32069
(904) 427-5674

The image above is an advertisement from a yearbook for Charley Baldwin's first shop, just steps from the ocean on Flagler Avenue. He started making short boards in a warehouse in nearby Edgewater. One Smyrna Surfari Club member remembers seeing Charley paddle out at the inlet, ecstatic, on the very first board he ever shaped and how proud Charley was. The photograph is from the local newspaper. Charley's face is a familiar one around town, as after he sold his shops he went into real estate. (Courtesy of the Smyrna Surfari Club.)

Surfers are loyal to their shaper and vice versa. Gene Varano seems proud of and satisfied with his Richenberg thruster. Several local shapers have popped up in New Smyrna Beach over the last couple of decades, many through admiration for the work of master shapers. (Courtesy of the Smyrna Surfari Club.)

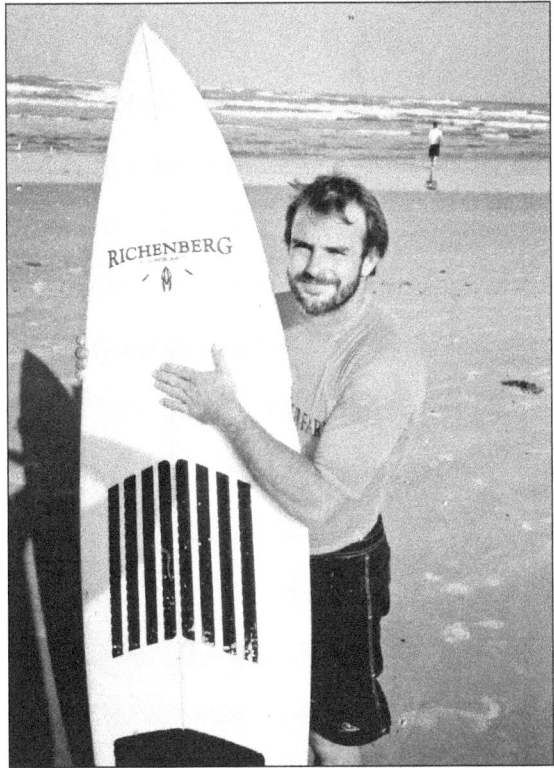

Master shapers do not have to be generous with their skills, time, and equipment, but Randy Richenberg is. Here a New Smyrna High senior assesses his senior project in Randy's factory in nearby Edgewater. Shaping requires talent, patience, and dedication. Few become masters at the art. (Author's collection.)

Seen here is a great pose of Charley Baldwin from his high school yearbook in 1968. This is long before Charley would own a lucrative surf shop in town or would begin shaping his CB-label boards. Notice the *Endless Summer* poster in the background. Buddy Wright has a copy autographed by Robert August. (Courtesy of Rusty Davis.)

This advertisement for CB surfboards features team rider Clyde Rodgers far from New Smyrna Beach but captures nicely (with the inset of Charley Baldwin carefully sanding a rail) the necessary relationship between hot surfers and the shapers behind them. Team riders get boards for free and advertise with their surfing. (Courtesy of Charley Baldwin.)

Five

WORLD'S SAFEST BATHING BEACH?

As has been seen from the advertisements for New Smyrna Beach—Coronado Beach—as far back as the 1940s, it was billed as "the World's Safest Bathing Beach." Those who grew up here have always understood this comes from an understanding of and respect for the sea and her wiles, paired with a world-class lifesaving corps. Times have changed. Not only are some Volusia County Lifeguards now law enforcement officers, but New Smyrna has gained worldwide recognition as "Shark Bite Capital of the World." Can both be true?

As with any legend, myths abound. New Smyrna Beach's waters have always hosted sharks and lots of them. But there were not always hoards of swimmers and surfers in the water. It is important to note that New Smyrna Beach is the shark bite capital. They bite; they release. The waters of New Smyrna's inlet are murky and home to schools and schools of fish. A place with the legendary fishing of New Smyrna is bound to have legendary big fish. It does. Sharks are fish. They eat smaller fish. Years ago, Mrs. Feger, proprietress of a local seafood market, told the author as she was wrapping up a grouper purchase, "In a few years we are going to have a big, I mean really big, shark problem around here. They've banned gill nets for our fishermen. They used to kill lots of sharks caught in nets, now there's nothing out there to kill them. Mark my words, there's going to be shark bites with all those surfers at the inlet where the fish come and go." Listen to the fishwives. They have long been known for their wisdom.

At the local hospital, pink ladies say, there's a pool of cash contributed to by staff on a regular basis. The medical team that gets the next shark bite victim gets the pot. That said, New Smyrna can be safe for those who take precautions. Swim close to a lifeguard, hydrate, wear sunscreen, pay attention to the conditions. Know one's own limits and skill levels, watch the local surfers, and stay out of their way. They know what they are doing.

This drawing of Ponce Inlet from the New Smyrna side (note Ponce Lighthouse overlooking the gruesome scene) proves the local shark population is nothing new. Slaves pulled in and killed the fish. They were slaughtered for their livers and processed at the fishery located on the river side of the inlet where the U.S. Coast Guard Station stands today. The drawing seems accurate; the heaviest shark population in the area is still at the inlet, where currents bring fish, and bigger fish such as those in the illustration, into the river. Hammerhead, tiger, bull, nurse, black tip, spinner, shovelhead, sand, and even the occasional great white shark are found here. Despite worldwide media coverage, sharks are not new to the inlet at New Smyrna Beach. Several national publications have portrayed the recent rise in bites as a frightening phenomenon, when it is only a natural by-product of man's intrusion into the fishes' natural habitat. (Courtesy of the Southeast Volusia Historical Society.)

New Smyrna Beach is known world-wide for its fishing, as is nearby Edgewater. Anglers come from all over hoping for a catch like this one. This fellow had to hoist the fish with block and tackle; look at the size of the hook and rope. It was a catch to be proud of. (Courtesy of the Southeast Volusia Historical Society.)

This is the famous jumping shark accidentally photographed by surfer, artist, photographer, and native New Smyrnan Kem McNair. Said *Inside Edition* regarding the photograph, "The whole of the shark's body is clear of the water. 'I've had spinner sharks jump and land behind me when I was out surfing, and it will totally scare the pants off ya,' says McNair. New Smyrna Beach in Florida is known as the shark bite capital of the world. A total of 12 people have been bitten by sharks there so far this year." This photograph was taken in 2008. (Courtesy of Kem McNair.)

Kem McNair still has it—here he's in fine form at New Smyrna Inlet. (Photograph by Chad Shindoll, courtesy of Kem McNair.)

This paddleboard was made by Joanne Sikes's father for her and her siblings to paddle around in the river in Edgewater. Joanne donated it to the lifeguards; it was never actually used. Note the "Please bathe close to tower" sign on the tower. This still appears on the back of the Volusia County lifeguard towers, built in shop class at the local high schools. (Courtesy of the Southeast Volusia Historical Society.)

This picture shows bathers in early-20th-century costumes off New Smyrna Beach. These days, swimmers have to worry about a more grueling and deadly sun than they used to, but there is a lot more skin exposed by modern swimwear, as well. (Courtesy of the Southeast Volusia Historical Society.)

On the back of this picture is penciled only "Pontiac 8, 7/4/39." One advantage for lifeguards, then and now, is that driving on New Smyrna's wide, white sand beaches makes it possible to move rapidly to and from emergency situations. Modern lifeguards have trucks, jet skis, and Zodiacs. (Courtesy of the Southeast Volusia Historical Society.)

This photograph, taken about 1940, shows women lifeguards at New Smyrna Beach. The rowboat behind them has given way to more modern equipment, but lifeguards still need other skills to do their job well, such as sharp eyes, excellent swimming skills, emergency preparedness training, and the ability to avoid distractions and the lull of boredom from long hours on a tower in the hot sun. (Courtesy of the Southeast Volusia Historical Society.)

The old New Smyrna Beach lifeguard tower has been replaced with a more modern version in the same location, just south of the Flagler Avenue beach ramp. Behind it can be seen the public restroom and shower facilities and the front of the lifeguard station. (Courtesy of the Southeast Volusia Historical Society.)

This vintage photograph, probably pre–World War II, shows two lifeguards sharing a tower and keeping an eye on the water. Usually there is one guard per tower, but occasionally beachgoers will see a "double tower" or two-seater. Although towers are now painted red, the design, including a hole in the seat for an umbrella, has not changed over the years. There are wheels on two legs of the tower, and the guard must heft and wheel the tower up and down the beach depending on tides and well past the high tide mark at the end of a shift. Nowadays, with hundreds of people on the beach and in the water, it is quite a job to keep everyone safe. Chalkboards on the back of the towers and color-coded flags keep visitors informed of current conditions. (Courtesy of the Southeast Volusia Historical Society.)

73

This jetty, constructed decades ago by the Army Corps of Engineers on the south side of the inlet, is a favorite spot for anglers. It is also the subject of hot debate around town, as it has been a trial-and-error project that contributed to the inlet's now world-renowned surf. (Courtesy of the Southeast Volusia Historical Society.)

Six

GROMMETS

"Everybody loves a grommet," is a saying in the surfing world. Grommets are the kids who hang around the beach, waiting for anything that even resembles a wave. They idolize experienced surfers, swap surf tales, paddle out together, and generally have a good time, honing their skills and finding out exactly what kind of surfers they will be. Some compete, and some do not. They seem to run in packs and sport shaggy, salty, messy hair and sun burnt noses. Usually they figure out one surf shop to patronize and pester the employees and generally hang around when they are not in the water. One of the great things about New Smyrna is that parents of the grommets know that the older locals always keep an eye out for them in and out of the water, and the kids know it too. A few show early promise as competitors and show up for every contest they can. Most are short boarders, showing off on tiny surfboards, and a very few idolize the longboarders and surf "old school." Sometimes they take a little ribbing. Some of them body board, and almost all of them sidewalk surf, or skateboard, when they cannot be in the water. Gromms can be very determined in getting to the surf. For example, a couple of years ago, Natalie Varano, 11 years old, was invited to accompany friends on a trip to Oahu. She quickly saved more than enough money to pay for her trip and brought some New Smyrna moves to Ala Moana, Kahana Bay, Crouching Lion, and Barber's Point.

As well loved as grommets are, kooks are frowned upon. A kook is someone who wants to be a surfer but does not know what they are doing and does not bother to learn. One of the reasons kooks are disliked is because when they get in the water without the proper skills and knowledge they can be dangerous. Surfing at New Smyrna Inlet is a privilege earned, and more than one grommet has been a little nervous on his or her first paddle out there. Respect is the golden rule, and as long as they have that, they do okay.

Evan Magee and Scott Baggett watch a heat at a contest in the late 1970s. (Courtesy of Evan Magee.)

Perhaps too old to be called grommets, here is the Twenty-seventh Avenue surf syndicate—from left to right, Tom Carlson, Brian Van Winkle, Mike Martin, and Ken Carlson—caught doing some back-porch modification to a surfboard. Most ding repair in those days was done at home. Surfers could not just run down to a local shop for help—there were not any. (Courtesy of Mike Martin.)

Older surfers keep an eye on the kids, and this photograph of a late 1970s group at the inlet typifies that. Seen here are, from left to right, Mike Coln, Ed Bartlett, Scott Bauer, Eric Coln, Carl Truesdell, and Bob Minasi. Surfing is also often a family activity. Carl lived close to the Colns and married Mike and Eric's sister Marie. (Courtesy of Carl Truesdell.)

Seen here is the making of a grommet: Marie and Carl Truesdell with their toddler, Mitchell. From the looks of him, Mitch has just been out for a surf lesson. In New Smyrna, some of the youngest surfers start learning from their parents. (Courtesy of Carl Truesdell.)

In this teachable moment, Kate Cumiskey responds to niece Julia's request to learn some "rad moves" in Dan and Diane Hughes's side yard. Kids often express an interest in surfing before they are out of diapers. (Courtesy of Laura Duran Davis.)

John Davis is showing some fundamentals to his daughter, Julia, but she is more interested in the outside break—a good sign. This rainy afternoon off Bethune Beach featured long lines and a nice off-shore wind. (Courtesy of Laura Duran Davis.)

This photograph of Gene Varano with his daughter, Natalie, at the inlet illustrates, as perhaps no other in this book can, the spirit of surfing in New Smyrna Beach. Most parents here want their children to learn water safety very, very early. Respect for the ocean is crucial. Children learn early to surf in groups and to pay attention to everything going on in the water, on the shore, and in the sky above. While Gene has been surfing the inlet since he was a child and his wife Suzanne is a nationally ranked champion, the "most supreme pleasure" cited in the introduction to this book is what it is all about. What a gift to pass that on to one's children. Gene and Suzanne's children, Wes, Ben, and Nat, all surf. How could they not? (Courtesy of Suzanne Varano.)

Toddlers make their own fun at a Surfari contest under the watchful eyes of mothers, members, and the Volusia County Beach patrol. During heats, kids needed to stay out of the water. Most of the Surfari contests take place "out front" at Flagler Avenue, though some are still held at the inlet. (Courtesy of the Smyrna Surfari Club.)

Two grommets are seen here with trophies from a Surfari contest. One of the best things about the Surfari contests is that they bring out competitors of all age ranges and skill levels, and everyone always has fun, including the Surfaris working at the contest. Traditionally a party follows that night at Clancy's Cantina. (Courtesy of the Smyrna Surfari Club.)

This picture of surfing contestants and the crowd is most likely from the late 1970s, judging by the surfboards, station wagon in the background, clothing, and hairstyles. However, it could just as easily be the present day. It is a typical post-contest beach scene; these days there are contests on a regular basis. (Courtesy of Mike Martin.)

This grommet practices cross stepping on his nose rider on a small winter's afternoon at the inlet. Unlike the pioneers, he has had plenty of longboarders before him to watch and learn from. Grommets spend a lot of time deciding which wave-riding vehicles to use, then perfecting their skills on favorite boards. (Author's collection.)

Scott Baggett moved to New Smyrna Beach from Alabama as a youngster and quickly took to the water. He is still here. (Courtesy of Evan Magee.)

The caption for this yearbook photograph reads, "Jason Preskitt, Todd Perry, Lindsey Baldwin, and Marcie Baldwin (not shown) enjoy a day at Bethune Beach. They enjoyed the day with big smiles on their burnt faces." Kids often hang out at the beach together after school. (Courtesy of New Smyrna Beach High School.)

This is a photograph of the New Smyrna Beach Junior High School surf club; the year is 1976. Teacher Gordon Smith is the sponsor, and there are 12 members. The surf club would do beach cleanups and community service events as well as getting together to surf. (Author's collection.)

By the time the new middle school was completed, eight years later, the surf club had tripled in size—there are 36 members. The sponsor that year was teacher Michael Purpura. The same activities applied; the group would perform community service projects, including beach cleanups, and go surfing together. (Courtesy of Carol Ann Davis.)

When they cannot be in the water for one reason or another, young surfers often pull out their skateboards. In former days, skateboards served as a great mode of transportation. Although skating on the streets or sidewalks of New Smyrna Beach is currently illegal, they can still skate in driveways. (Author's collection.)

Jimmy Cumiskey practices a hang five on his Luke Nosewalker, a Sector 9 skateboard, on Robinson Road on the north beach. He is probably wishing he were in the water but could not find anyone to surf with. When this photograph was taken, skateboarding had not yet been banned on Florida streets. (Author's collection.)

Marshall Hughes tips his hat to his buddies from the top of the quarter pipe in his driveway. Marshall is a talented surfer and photographer. Since the skating ban on streets and sidewalks, kids have had to get creative with where they can skate. (Courtesy of Marshall Hughes.)

Colton Snowden kills time until he and his friends can get a ride to the inlet. Grommets often hang out together, waiting around for a lift to the inlet or permission to go surf. Some rig up racks on the back of their beach cruisers (bicycles) and tow their boards to the beach. (Courtesy of Marshall Hughes.)

Seen here is Natalie Varano on a fast right at the Haven, a surf spot south of the inlet on a cold winter afternoon in 2008. Natalie, like her dad, surfs goofy foot. There was a storm coming that afternoon, and the waves jacked up for a couple of hours; everyone flocked to the beach. (Author's collection.)

This is a shot of Mike Clancy with one of his first surfboards, a Campbell built in Melbourne, Florida. Doug Haut, the great Santa Cruz shaper, shaped this board and still shapes boards for Mike, since he now lives in the Santa Cruz area. (Courtesy of Mike Clancy.)

Seven

THE SMYRNA SURFARI CLUB

The Smyrna Surfari Club has been actively promoting the image of surfing in the community since 1979. How successful they have been. Here surfing is respected for what it is, a healthy sport that brings money, notoriety, and even artistry to town. But visibility is not the only concern of the Surfaris. With members who are the bedrock of the business community, they have successfully preserved the local environs through activism and service while defending the beach access needed for the sport. That access makes New Smyrna a popular destination for families across the state and even the nation.

The Smyrna Surfari Club holds beach cleanups and raises funds with contests for the annual scholarships they give at the local high school. Club members organize and run the contests—they even make the trophies. For some kids, a Surfari trophy is more of a prize than a highly visible, publicized win from a national organization. National ratings pale in comparison to the respect of the local icons, as can be seen from the smiles on the faces of some of the Surfari winners. Plus, these contests are pure fun. The Halloween Spooktackular even has a surfing costume contest, which gets more outrageous on an annual basis.

The club holds monthly meetings at the Boat and Ski Club, a low concrete-block structure on the edge of the Indian River. There are several parties a year, with live music and seafood galore. Grommets play on the shore and race between their parents. The Surfaris have been around long enough to see the academic and business successes of many of their scholarship recipients. And most of them are still surfing.

This is the original membership photograph of the Smyrna Surfari Club, taken in 1979. It is captioned "Chairman: Tom Wright, Secretaries: Gordon Smith & Mike Martin, Treasurer: Gordon Smith." (Courtesy of the Smyrna Surfari Club.)

SMYRNA SURFARI CLUB INC.

We . . .

- Give an annual Scholarship to an eligible High School Senior.

- Have offered over $30,000 in Scholarships for area surfers

- Promote and Defend reasonable Beach Access for the sport of Surfing.

- We have been actively promoting the image of surfing in our community since 1979.

- Have fought for environmental issues that affect our sport and lifestyle.

- Sponsor and Promote Two Annual Surf Contests in conjunction with the Eastern Surfing Association, to help raise the standard of surfing in our area.

- Hold Surf Contests against other area Surf Clubs in a Fun Family atmosphere.

- Hold monthly meetings to discuss the latest in Surfing and plan for upcoming events on our schedule.

Have at least Two Parties a Year that bring together our members and their families to celebrate our Club Achievements and Florida Lifestyle.

IF YOU HAVE ANY INTEREST IN JOINING THE SMYRNA SURFARI CLUB, PLEASE CONTACT OUR CLUB AT:
P.O. Box 2362
New Smyrna Beach, Florida 32170
or Call
Rick Tresher (904) _____ or Bob Keeth (904)_____

This is an early brochure promoting the Smyrna Surfari Club. Despite what may appear on first blush to be a purely recreational organization, the club is anything but. Surfing and surfers have a long history of being misunderstood. One of the main goals of the club is to dispel myths about surfing and "promote the image of surfing." Why is this important? Prejudice equals ignorance. Ignorance is dispelled through education, and the Smyrna Surfari Club has done an outstanding job over its 30 years of educating the community. Members range in profession from doctorates in environmental science, to exceptional student education teachers, to professional surfers, to bankers, to pilots, to business owners. These people are the bedrock of the town. In the early days of surfing in New Smyrna, the pioneers had to fight ignorance to be able to surf. Now surfing has brought money, culture, and class to town. (Courtesy of the Smyrna Surfari Club.)

Mike Clancy is seen here on a bottom turn on a small day in the early 1970s. By this time, Mike was a highly decorated local lifeguard. (Courtesy of Mike Clancy.)

Competitors in the annual Spooktackular Costume Contest pose for a shot for the newspaper. Local kids and adults have a great deal of good clean fun with this event. That is world-class, up-and-coming surfer Nils Schweizer in the cow suit. Professional surfers here support their community. That is part of what makes this town so special. (Courtesy of the Smyrna Surfari Club.)

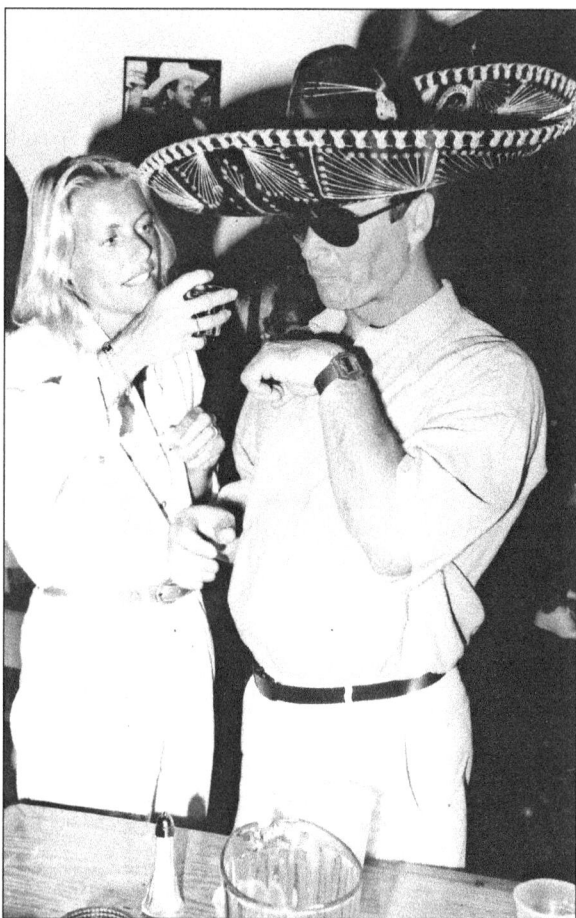

Jennifer Baldwin and Rocky Jowers are clowning at Clancy's Cantina after a long day of working a Surfari contest. Clancy's is the official restaurant of the club, giving time, donations, and space generously over the years. Owners and twins Matt Clancy and Margaret Mickelbrink are Surfaris and leaders in the community. (Courtesy of the Smyrna Surfari Club.)

TO WHOM IT MAY CONCERN:

    It was presented and passed, that a Beach Party be held on the 23 day of April.

    This gathering of the elite group will be held at the Bowl, from 7:30 till you're strong enough to walk home, we sure don't want you to drive.

    Girls, bring plenty to eat, food too. Boys, bring drinks and blankets, to keep things hot.

    Keep this party quiet, unless you want slobs and cops there.

                    YOUR SOCIAL DIRECTORS

This mimeographed invitation to an early surf party cites a couple of New Smyrna treasures gone with the wind: the Bowl, which was a deep depression between tall sand dunes at the inlet and is now inaccessible due to development (condominiums), and nighttime beach driving. It is actually, as is easy to tell, tongue in cheek. (Courtesy of Buddy Wright.)

Former Surfari Club president Sonny Yambor is far from home. Many New Smyrna surfers travel occasionally for waves, but if asked, to a surfer, New Smyrna remains home. (Courtesy of Sonny Yambor.)

Seen here is founding Surfari Club member Buddy Wright, one of Mike Martin's heroes in early-day New Smyrna Beach. Buddy is styling with a beautiful cheater five—he makes it look not only fun but also easy. Buddy was a founding member of the Smyrna Surf Club as well as the Surfari. (Courtesy of Buddy Wright.)

Surfari Club members Mike Martin (left) and Randy Schwoerer present Gary Schwoerer with the Smyrna Surfari Club Scholarship. It is a good day when one can present his little brother with a scholarship. Anyone with even a hint of family relationship with a candidate is excused from voting for the winner. Surfaris have given thousands to deserving surfers over the years. (Courtesy of the Smyrna Surfari Club.)

This is the boardwalk at Flagler Avenue where the Surfari Club holds most of its contests. Although it has been rebuilt since this late 1970s photograph was taken, it is up for another rebuild currently. The more things change, the more they stay the same—there is still girl watching. (Courtesy of Southeast Volusia Historical Society.)

Surfari member Frank Marshall wrote, "I believe that this is Fall 1983. It was early morning at the inlet and somewhat overcast. Steve Burkhalter had a friend with a telephoto lens and he sat up on one of the dunes and took some pictures of Steve and also of some of his friends (that's where I came in). The 2 pictures are of the same wave and they are a continuation, I guess, not a sequence because the second picture shows me coming off the bottom of the wave after making the first turn backside left, then coming off the top to end up in the position of making the bottom turn under the breaking wave, still going backside left. I remember it as a very glassy day, about shoulder-high, with only about 8 or 10 guys in the water because it was early. It was a nice Fall north swell, and a lot of fun that morning." (Courtesy of Dr. Frank Marshall.)

Here is a Smyrna Surfari Club member photograph. The sun is in their eyes, so this is a morning shot, most likely before a contest. Noble Bilby holds a "Smyrna Surfari Club" surfboard. Gordon Smith, ever the prankster, holds bunny ears behind a friend's head. Though Gordon is active at nearly every Surfari event, he is essentially private, and few surfing photographs of him exist. (Courtesy of the Smyrna Surfari Club.)

This is the ceremony installing the monument at Flagler Avenue on the boardwalk at which Mike Martin so eloquently spoke—his speech was used as the introduction of this book. Shaped by Charley Baldwin (leaning on the monument, wearing sunglasses), this first monument was destroyed by a hurricane in 2004. The plaque was recovered and is now mounted on the third and hopefully last version of the monument. (Courtesy of the Smyrna Surfari Club.)

96

Eight

THE PROFESSIONALS

This chapter, dedicated to surfing professionals in New Smyrna Beach, is not about people who are winning contests right now, although New Smyrna boasts more of those than any other community in the world, including but not limited to Nils Schweitzer, Aaron Cormican, Jeremy and Caleb Johnston, Amy Nichol, and the Geiselman brothers. Open any surfing magazine, and at least one New Smyrna surfer can be in those pages. What other town can claim that? This chapter is about professionals in the surfing world, local and worldwide, and about people whose professional life is dedicated to surfing, like surf photographer and past champion Kem McNair; like shaper and community activist Randy Richenberg; like surf pro Jimmy Lane, who operates a surf school which teaches thousands of youngsters water safety and the intricate rules of surfing; like Mike Martin, a seminal figure in surfing worldwide and probably the most recognizable professional at the world-class events regulated by the Association of Surfing Professionals—and a New Smyrna Beach native.

The point is, New Smyrna professionals travel, but they always come home. And they trained in New Smyrna. They learned together and from each other, and they learned alone too, out on the consistently inconsistent surf available here. One of the reasons New Smyrna surfers, outside of their individual talents, go up handily against surfers from Hawaii, Australia, and California is that surf is sometimes so bad at New Smyrna Beach that they learn to surf on anything. There is something unnamable about this town that breeds these world-class individuals, right from the beginning with Charley Baldwin upsetting that cocky Hobie Team so long ago. And, thank God, it just keeps going.

This is Mike Martin's bio shot, somewhere in Australia on a rainy afternoon. Mike's work schedule with the Association of Surfing Professionals is grueling; he seems to be on the road more often than not. But Mike went out of the way to help with this book, so hats off to him. (Courtesy of Mike Martin.)

Slapping the lip on a local board shaped by Randy Schwoerer, Mike takes a little time off to have some fun at home. In this close-knit surfing community, it is not unusual to see someone as talented as Mike surfing "out front," showing the grommets how it is done. (Photograph by Sonny Yambor, courtesy of Mike Martin.)

smyrna surfers

Isobel McLaughlin
first place u.s. surfing championship
first place east coast surfing championship

Cathy McLaughlin
sixth place u.s. surfing championship
third place east coast surfing championship

This beautiful picture of champion Isabel McLaughlin and her sister, Cathy, comes from one of their high school yearbooks. World-class surfer Isabel sometimes surprises her students out in the lineup at the inlet. Isabel teaches marine biology at the local high school and is very private about her surfing history and abilities—although she cannot hide them in the water. The caption reads, "Isobel [sic] McLaughlin first place u.s. surfing championship, first place east coast surfing championship. Cathy McLaughlin sixth place u.s. surfing championship, third place east coast surfing championship." (That is before graduating from high school.) A brilliant teacher, Isabel has high expectations for her students, and they generally meet them. She also sponsored the yearbook for many years. Isabel is a perfect example of a surfing professional who is able to make a living in New Smyrna Beach. (Courtesy of New Smyrna Beach High School.)

This photograph of Isabel McLaughlin was found hanging on the wall of Inlet Charley's Surf Shop. It depicts a powerful roundhouse by a graceful surfer. One of the most wonderful things about this town is the legacy of surfers like Isabel and the practicality of young surfers watching with respect and learning. (Courtesy of Charley Baldwin.)

This photograph of Charley Baldwin on a surfboard of his own making absolutely captures the ease and fluid style that thrust him to the forefront of surfing from an early age. The loosely clasped hands behind his back make it look like getting shacked is the easiest thing in the world. Maybe it is for Charley. (Courtesy of Charley Baldwin.)

Jimmy Lane is paddling out in a heat. Jimmy dedicates his professional life to the youngsters of town, and they are happier, healthier, and safer for it. Running a surf school has got to be a harrowing job, but he keeps at it year after year. He is also an accomplished artist. (Courtesy of the Smyrna Surfari Club.)

"Big R," Randy Richenberg, is seen here, somewhere tropical. Randy travels occasionally to surf, but as his obligations to the city demand as city commissioner and vice mayor, he spends most of his time right here in New Smyrna Beach. He also has his hands full keeping Richenberg Surfboards running smoothly. Still Randy found time to help out with this book. (Courtesy of Randy Richenberg.)

Here is a look at the inside of a shaping room, the area in a factory where surfboards are made, or "shaped." The shaper is Randy Richenberg, sometimes called "Big R." Shaping is an art requiring not only practice and hard work but also talent. There are now machines that can imitate shapers, but most surfers scoff at machine-shaped boards, unless that machine is guided by the hands of a master like Randy. Then, admittedly, some pretty cool innovations can happen. However, the bumper sticker on Randy's truck typifies surfers' attitudes toward mass-produced boards. It reads "Friends don't let friends ride China boards." (Both from author's collection.)

One of the things Mike Martin enjoys about his job is being on a first name basis with the best surfers in the world, year after year. Tom Curren (left) and Mike are Scrabble partners. Ian Cairns asked Mike in the 1980s to write the rule book for surfing. "The world surfs by New Smyrna rules," Mike said in an interview for this book. (Courtesy of Mike Martin.)

Pete Townend laughs as Mike has his first taste of kava, an age-old herbal drink that was the beverage of choice for the royal families of the South Pacific. Kava grows abundantly in the sun-drenched islands of Polynesia. Although drunk for centuries by the islanders, it was during Capt. James Cook's voyage when white man first encountered the plant and its consumption in sacred ceremonies. (Courtesy of Mike Martin.)

HUNTINGTON BEACH SURFING WALK OF FAME

INAUGURAL INDUCTIONS - AUGUST 4, 1994

This brochure for the Hunting Beach Surfing Walk of Fame inaugural inductions on August 4, 1994, in California featured none other than Smyrna Surf Club. Skipper Eppelin is in the coffee ring in the center. New Smyrna's own Gordon Smith is just under the "ton" in the logo. (Courtesy of Buddy Wright.)

Mike Doyle, Robert Wolfe, and Robert August—of *Endless Summer* fame—hoist the copy of the Smyrna Surf Club photograph that hangs in the surf museum in California. The irony of New Smyrna boys on their brochure is not lost on these three; the arc of the surfing world spans a continent. (Courtesy of Buddy Wright.)

Nine

FREESURFING

Freesurfing is surfing without the pressure of performing. The divide is sometimes wide between freesurfers and competitors, although competitors are not bound to be working all the time. But aren't they? Some surfers have told me a point came in their surfing life where they deliberately turned from the limelight back to their roots; surfing for surfing's sake alone. Contests can be cutthroat, as this anecdote from a local contest relates: Two grommets were standing at the water's edge, waiting for their heat to start. They'd never met. One said to the other, "How long have you been surfing?" The youngster replied, "Six weeks," with a friendly smile. "I've been surfing six years. I'm going to kick your butt." "Good luck!" came the warm and heartfelt reply. He did not care if he won; he was just there to have fun. The other was already a jaded competitor. Ironically the newer surfer won the day, and a new surfboard, his first. Contests can ruin kids but can also drive a surfer to hone their skills. It depends on the surfer. Some thrive on competition, while some cannot stand it.

One of the things learned in writing this book is that surfing is necessary to the people who do it. On September 9, 2009, Kelly Slater (nine time world champion and Floridian) made a guest appearance on "Wait, Wait, Don't Tell Me," a National Public Radio show. The host asked what he was like when he couldn't get in the water. Kelly likened it to an addict experiencing withdrawals. There are surfers for whom surfing is almost a part of their body. You can see it when you watch them; this is an organic thing. They're fluid, spiritual surfers and almost universally shy, quiet people: like Mike Martin, like Isabel McLaughlin—those who deliberately chose to turn away from the limelight. Not always, though. Sometimes for a surfer it is as necessary as breathing, and they compete. It is a lovely thing indeed.

This beautiful snapshot from the 1968 high school yearbook captures the spirit of the solitary surfer. This could be anyone. That is sunrise over the water at New Smyrna Beach, the dawn of a new day. What could be more spiritual than the ocean on a summer morn? (Courtesy of Rusty Davis.)

This is another yearbook photograph from the early days. As can be seen from the surfer walking out, those boards were heavy. But surfers took good care of their equipment, and boards were "glassed" (polyester resin–impregnated fiberglass) heavily due to the fact that surfers squatted on their knees to paddle out. (Courtesy of Rusty Davis.)

Somehow in the earliest days of surfing in New Smyrna Beach it seemed easier and freer. There was an innocence to those days of discovery that is sadly lost on most of the surfers today. That line in the picture is simply someone's pencil line when he wanted to claim this anonymous yearbook picture from 1968. (Courtesy of Rusty Davis.)

Here is a beautiful shot of early boards (they were not called longboards then, just surfboards) by Steve Nielsen of his wife, Geri. These would fetch thousands each today in the condition that they are in this photograph. (Courtesy of Buddy Wright.)

Seen here is Suzanne Hunter at Bethune Beach in the mid-1960s. This photograph is from Mike Martin's personal photograph album. Suzanne was one of the first women to surf New Smyrna Beach. (Courtesy of Mike Martin.)

This is an awesome shot of Buddy Wright deep in the tube at "Main Street" (Flagler Avenue) in the late 1960s. See how many surfers are in the water? Once those guys brought surfing to town, New Smyrna would never be the same. (Courtesy of Buddy Wright.)

This is another shot from Mike's personal album, showing his friend Ken Carlson at Bethune Beach. Bethune is about 5 miles south of Main Street and was the back of beyond in those days. (Courtesy of Mike Martin.)

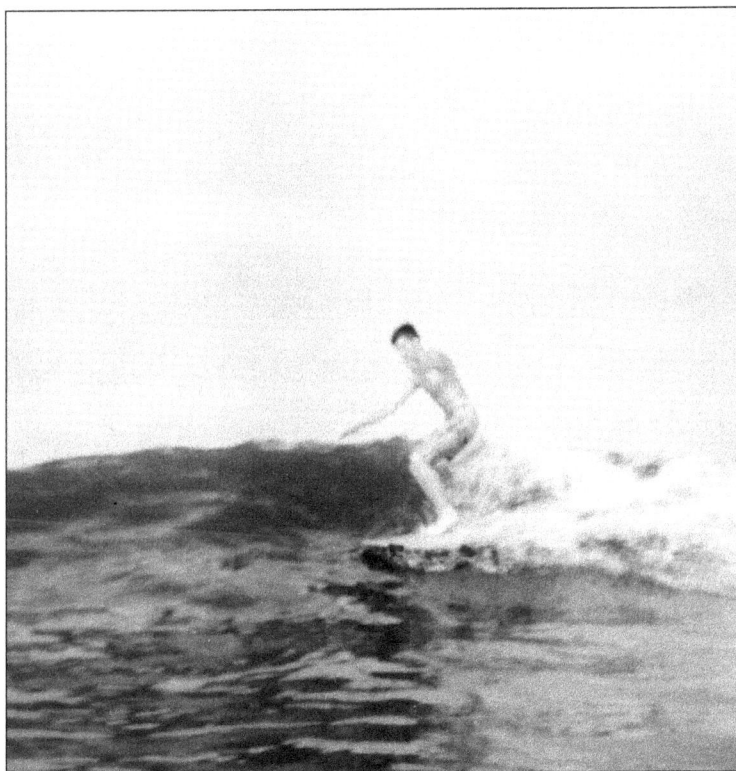

Ken's twin brother Tom walks to the nose in the mid-1960s at Fifteenth Street. These shots were taken with a Polaroid camera, now obsolete. (Courtesy of Mike Martin.)

Mike Martin is pictured on a winter day in New Smyrna Beach. (Photograph by Sonny Yambor, courtesy of Mike Martin.)

Joe Surbaugh is seen in this image absolutely ripping at New Smyrna Inlet. How can a surfer fail to defer to a move like that? The primary rule of competition (keeping in mind Joe is not competing here) is an original of Mike Martin's: when two surfers take off on a wave together, the surfer on the inside, closest to the curl, gets the wave. That is a "New Smyrna rule." (Courtesy of Randy Richenberg.)

Thomas Wheeler is pictured as a grommet on a chilly day at New Smyrna Inlet. Thomas surfed for Charley Baldwin, which made him a team rider. (Courtesy of Thomas Wheeler.)

A young Evan Magee is seen here at New Smyrna Beach in the 1980s. Notice the "TEAM" on the board below Richenberg. Randy was Evan's shaper and sponsor. (Courtesy of Evan Magee.)

Quiet people make some of the finest surfers. Here James Guzman is pictured in perfect flight. James is one of the quietest people the author has ever known; they went all the way through school together. But there is no doubt he's at home in the water. To quote Mike Martin, James is "One of the most powerful surfers ever from N.S.B. We as judges used to call him 'Slugman.'" (Courtesy of Randy Richenberg.)

This is an absolutely breathtaking shot of Suzanne Varano shooting the pier at Lake Worth in south Florida. Suzanne is a champion surfer and old friend (from high school) of Kate Whatley, director of Christian Surfers New Smyrna Beach Chapter. Suzanne surfs whenever she has the opportunity, and her talents and the talents of her husband, Gene, are hopefully rubbing off on her progeny, Wes, Ben, and Natalie. Suzanne and Gene are charter members of the Surfari Club and live steps from the beach on the north beach. (Courtesy of Suzanne Varano.)

This is a snapshot of Mike Clancy with a board from the late 1960s. This picture, more than most in this book, gives a good glimpse of what the houses and terrain look like on the island of New Smyrna Beach. The road behind Mike, A1A or Atlantic Avenue, is now five lanes in some places, and few of the homes facing the Atlantic Ocean survive in their original shape, replaced by much larger homes or condominiums. (Courtesy of Mike Clancy.)

This is a picture of Mike on the way out for a session at Bethune Beach in the spring of 1972. The board is a 7-6 Gordon and Smith Magic Model. (Courtesy of Mike Clancy.)

Mike Clancy is seen here in Nicaragua in 2007. Many surfers who cut their teeth on New Smyrna Beach's consistently inconsistent surf hold their own around the world. (Courtesy of Mike Clancy.)

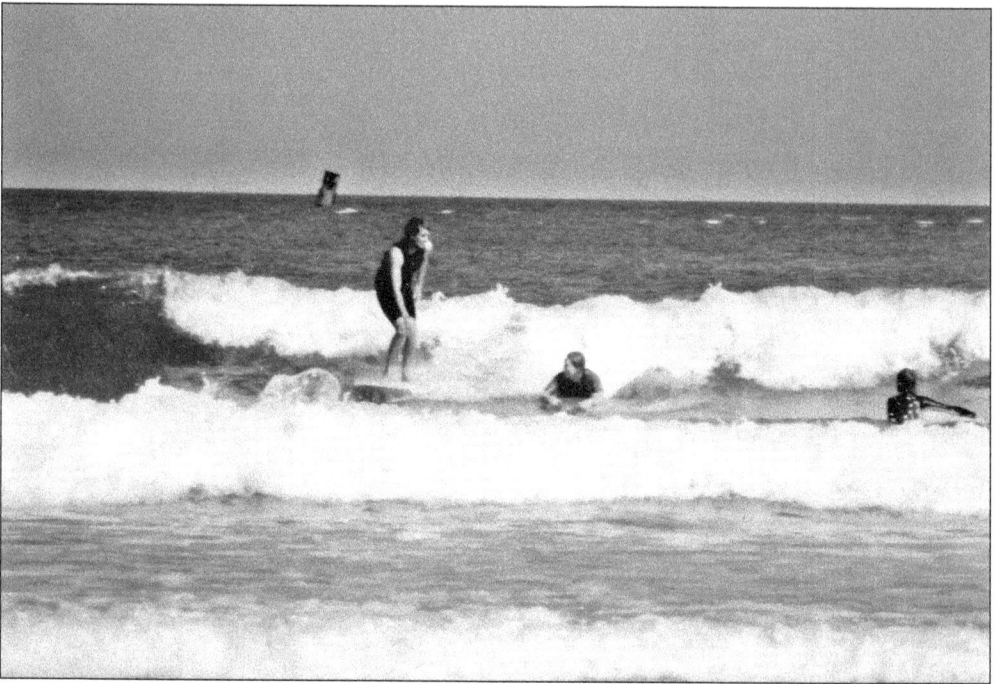

That is the inlet buoy in the background; on big days, the surf breaks all the way out to the buoy. It is a good thing when surfing is a family activity. Here kids are seen paddling out to surfer on a wave next to his spouse on a body board. A good time was had by all. (Author's collection.)

Mike Martin is seen in this image taking a break from work to have a little fun with what started it all, displaying the organic style of surfers who devote a lifetime to it. There is something for the rest of us to envy in an ability to do a thing this well. (Courtesy of Mike Martin.)

New Smyrna surfers are seen here in Paradise, Oahu, at dawn in June 2008. Comdr. Phil Davis, center, was the 1984 recipient of the Smyrna Surfari Club Scholarship. It paid for his dorm the first semester at Georgia Tech. A native of New Smyrna Beach, he grew up on Robinson Road, pictured below. One New Smyrna grommet said while walking along the shore at Wiamea that he was not surprised when he ran into two girls from his 11th-grade English class. It is, after all, a small world. (Author's collection.)

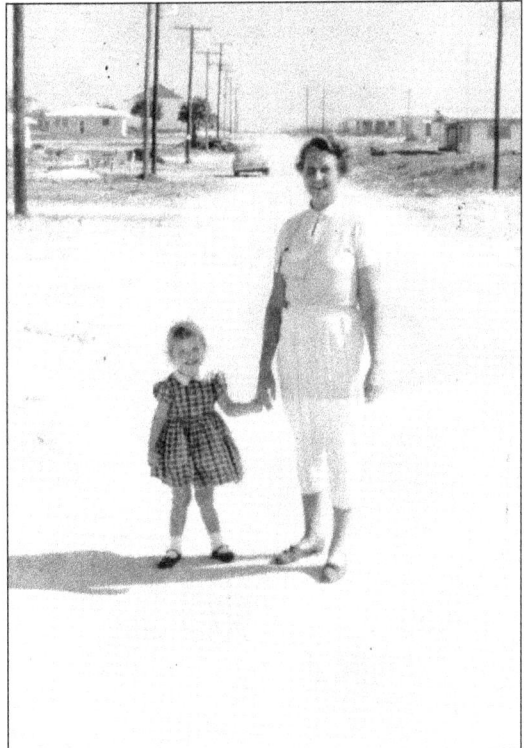

Gwen Gold stands with her grandmother, Katherine Pierre, outside the Gold home at the west end of Robinson Road. The Davis home is to the right midway down the street, which terminates at the Atlantic Ocean. This is the narrowest part of the island. The break at the end of Robinson Road is "home break" to Surfari Scholarship winners Wes Cich, Thomas Wheeler, Evan Magee, Philip Davis, and Mikel Cumiskey Jr. and now to Mike Martin as well. (Courtesy of Lynn Pierre Schaefer.)

On a perfect winter afternoon at his home break at the end of Robinson Road, Mikel Cumiskey Jr. is in New Smyrna for a visit from Bellingham, Washington. A February day here is balmy compared to one in the Pacific Northwest, where he and his girlfriend, Kelsi Johnson, make their home. (Courtesy of Kelsi Johnson.)

This is a shot of Evan Magee "back in the day," while the one below is current. It is great when surfers manage to remain in their hometown, although Evan, like other New Smyrnans, often travels for surf. Evan lives on Robinson Road. (Courtesy of Evan Magee.)

Local youngsters sometimes make fun of the standup paddleboarders, calling them "janitors of the sea" because of the sweeping motions they make using their paddles. However, one needs to spend only a few minutes watching Evan Magee to realize this takes both strength and skill. (Courtesy of Evan Magee.)

Surfing inside the rocks is not advisable, but sometimes it is irresistible. Shaman Burton is having a good time. Surfers joke that inside the rocks they, "paddle with their pinkies." Actually their dangling feet are in just as much, if not more, danger from nipping sharks. (Courtesy of Shaman Burton.)

Shaman Burton slaps that lip on his CB. There are two jetties, one on the north, or Daytona, side, and one on the south, or New Smyrna Beach, side of the inlet into the Indian River. It is pretty gutsy to surf there—or foolish, according to some surf moms—but Shaman could not resist. (Courtesy of Shaman Burton.)

This is a vintage photograph of Charles Hall. Charles also appears in the charter Surfari Club photograph. (Courtesy of Mimi Hall.)

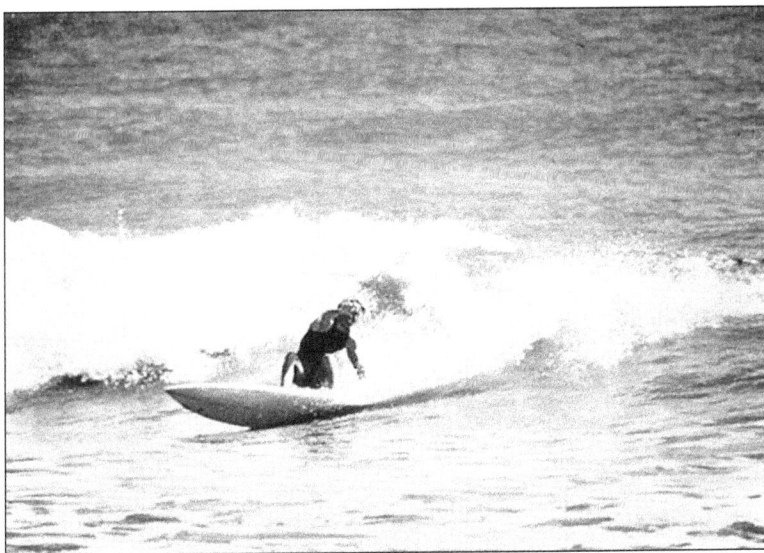

This photograph of New Smyrna Beach High School graduate Lonnie Low was taken by Pat Altes in the summer of 1979. (Courtesy of Lonnie Low.)

As said before, New Smyrna surfers travel. While in graduate school for architecture, 1985 Surfari Scholarship winner Thomas Wheeler lived in Los Angeles but travelled to Mexico, Puerto Rico, the Bahamas, and throughout California to surf. In high school, Tom made several trips to Cape Hatteras, North Carolina. In 1981 and 1983, he competed in the Eastern Surfing Association and surfed for Inlet Charley's Surf Team. The top picture was taken in Puerto Escondido, Mexico, in 1985. The bottom picture is from Punta Roca, El Salvador, in 2004. (Both courtesy of Thomas Wheeler.)

This is a beautiful picture of 1979 New Smyrna Beach High School graduate Dan Hughes, father of excellent photographer Marshall Hughes, whose photographs appear in the Grommets chapter of this book. Dan grew up surfing at Fifteenth Street but now lives on the north beach with his wife, Diane, and their children. North beach is north of Flagler Avenue. (Courtesy of Dan Hughes.)

Sometimes on a chilly day at the inlet, if one is lucky, it is not too crowded. Evan Magee grew up surfing here, and he still has it. Evan trades up his stand up paddleboard for a thruster (a type of short board) in this photograph. (Courtesy of Evan Magee.)

Geri Nielsen is seen here stepping out of her Volkswagen Beetle at New Smyrna Beach in 1964. Driving on the beach has always been one of the town's main attractions for visitors. In 1964, the beach was open to cars 24/7, but it is now closed at sunset and opened at 8:00 in the morning. (Courtesy of Buddy Wright.)

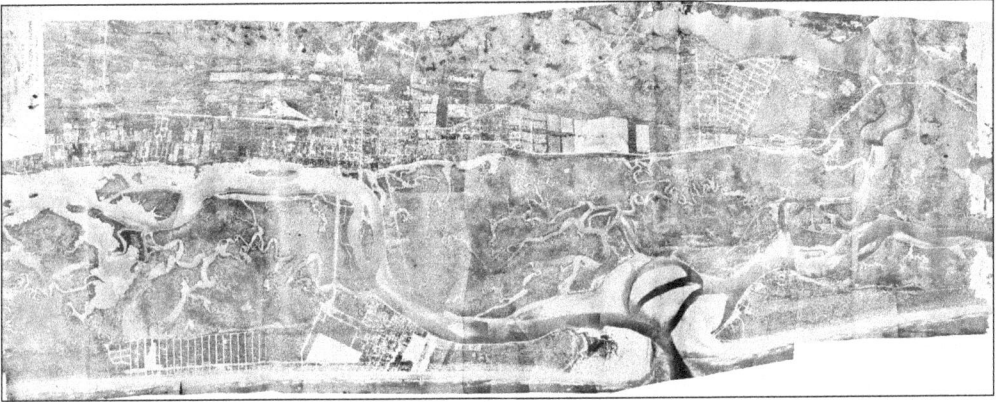

The photograph above shows the island, mainland, inlet, river, and marshes of New Smyrna Beach. Although the main surfing area for locals is south of the inlet, there are breaks all along the beach. Below is a photograph looking west into the inlet. New Smyrna is to the left. (Both courtesy of Sonny Yambor.)

On these last pages are a few parting images. This is the view of a storm rolling in from the north at the boardwalk at the end of Sapphire Avenue. That is one of the lifeguard towers made by high school students parked safely for the evening above the high-tide line. (Courtesy of Evan Magee.)

This is the view to the north across the inlet of Ponce Light. In days of tall ships, Ponce Inlet was a dangerous place, with shifting sandbars to run boats aground. Now a peaceful place in the late evening, a privileged few enjoy this view. (Author's collection.)

From left to right, Mickey Boucher, Buddy Wright, and Skipper Eppelin are obviously proud of their "new" surfboards in this 1962 photograph. Buddy's is a used balsawood "pop out," which was damaged in the nose (front tip) of the board before purchase and had to be shaved down and reshaped. (Courtesy of Buddy Wright.)

Visit us at
arcadiapublishing.com

www.ingramcontent.com/pod-product-compliance
Lightning Source LLC
Chambersburg PA
CBHW050559110426
42813CB00008B/2408